MY KIDS,
THE JOURNEY
OF A
LIVE-IN
NANNY

MY KIDS, THE JOURNEY OF A LIVE-IN NANNY

Carol Kelly

authorHOUSE®

AuthorHouse™ LLC
1663 Liberty Drive
Bloomington, IN 47403
www.authorhouse.com
Phone: 1-800-839-8640

Published by AuthorHouse 06/24/2014

ISBN: 978-1-4969-1919-9 (sc)
ISBN: 978-1-4969-1920-5 (e)

Library of Congress Control Number: 2014910973

Any people depicted in stock imagery provided by Thinkstock are models,
and such images are being used for illustrative purposes only.
Certain stock imagery © Thinkstock.

This book is printed on acid-free paper.

Dedication

"To my kids, I love you all more than words can ever say and there is no one on this earth that is more proud of you than me"

INTRODUCTION

As I sit watching my latest two kids eating their lunch, I think of all the experiences, people and places that have passed through my life. The children of course will always be a part of my life, as well as the homes I have lived in. If I sit back and concentrate I can almost picture every room in every house. Most of the houses still feel very much like home to me when I walk through the front door. It makes a person feel good to have so many homes, so many places where you can just sit and be yourself and chill out. I know that not all live in nannies have the same experience. I haven't either in all the homes I have lived in. I see myself as one of the lucky ones because I do feel at home in most of the houses. I mean I go to my Mom's house but I don't think of it as home, its just Mom's house. It might be different if she still lived in our hometown and in the house where I grew up. When all of this started I never dreamed that someday I would be looking back on a 24 year career. A career filled with so many little faces, giggles, hugs, kisses and first words. You are going to read those words a lot in this book, giggles, hugs, kisses and all, so get used to it. A huge sense of pride and overwhelming emotion fills me when I think about it. To think I have had an important role in so many little lives. Live-in nannies become part of families or at least I did. Live-in nannies become a friend and a confidant and a never-ending source of love and support for the kids and their parents. I hope that when you read this book you will have a better understanding of the nanny and her world. My hope for this book is parents and nannies will learn the importance of communication and understanding. I hope they both will learn to see things from both sides. This book is about my kids and our journey together and it is for all of the children in this country. I truly hope it can improve the image of the American nanny. I would love to see that image get back to that of

Mary Poppins. I know that sounds silly, but take a moment and think about what she did for that family. Now I am talking about the movie version not the book version, in the book version she is very different. But in the movie version, she taught that father how to be a Dad. She brought that family back together, remember in the end of the movie, they go skipping off into the sunset hand in hand. If we can get that image back then childcare in this country will improve and then you know what the future of this country improves, because the children are the future.

CHAPTER ONE

IN THE BEGINNING

In the 24 years that I have been a nanny some amazing, scary and very funny and wonderful things have happened. Several people whose opinion I value immensely said that I should write all my adventures down for people to read. They all said that it would make a great book. So for better or worse, let the adventure begin.

First things first I need to do is to give credit where credit is due. My love and desire to be what I am started with my grandmother. She was my father's mother and my Nana. Nana was my best friend when I was a little girl. I believe that she planted a seed in me so to speak a strong love for small children and especially babies. I will forever be in her debt for that I will always love and cherish her memory.

The actual nanny deal started in 1989. I was living and working in my hometown, Amarillo, Texas. For those of you who might not have had the great pleasure of being in the city of Amarillo, just let me say this about it. It is very flat, somewhat treeless and very windy most of the year. The best part of Amarillo is without question the people.

I was then a part of a wonderful group of Americans known as the working class poor. That is about everyone these day. I was working several jobs, as I still tend to do just to make ends meet. Those jobs included a pizza place, it had three locations in town. I worked at all three locations. I also took care of two unrelated children and worked in a small family run daycare. This was long before cell phones were available to the average person, so finding me was not always an easy task. My poor father had to find out the hard way several times.

Being a native Texan you understand, I had never heard of a quote unquote live in nanny. I remember watching Mary Poppins as a child and not really understanding exactly who she was and why the parents didn't take care of their own children. Never dreaming of course that I would someday live her life, sort of, I mean I wish I could make things magically appear out of my carpet bag, if I had one that is. Man, wouldn't a magic carpet bag come in handy sometimes!

Small town Amarillo was out of the loop when it came to nannies. Until one day in late 1989, I was looking in the want ads and there was this ad. A nanny placement agency had placed this ad about becoming a nanny. It promised great pay, travel and the chance to go to school. Wow, I thought a chance to do something I love to do care for children and get paid well and see more of this great country of ours. I don't have to tell you I jumped at the chance. I showed the ad to my Mom and asked her what she thought. She said that it was at least worth looking into and that it sounded exciting. The next day I made a phone call and started the ball rolling on my career as a nanny.

So after what seemed like tons and tons of paperwork and several interviews, the stage was set. I was told that parents would begin to call me. Parents did call from all over the country, but one struck a chord. It was a single mother with three young sons from Long Island New York. We must have talked for almost 3 hours over the phone, we had an instant connection. I didn't know then what I was myself into, but it's like they say hindsight is twenty/twenty. All I knew was that I was ready to get out of little old Amarillo. The sort of sad thing is now, I would give almost anything to go back to little old Amarillo and the simple life I had there. A couple of summers ago, I was on vacation with my family and we were in Texas passing through these small country towns. I found myself wishing that I could move there and enjoy the simple small town life again.

My father, God bless him, was not happy or excited about my decision. In some ways I had mixed feelings as well. The chance to see the world on one hand and my family on the other hand. What about my family? What about my grandmother, who depended on me for so very much? I had never lived away from home, away from Mom and Dad. How was I going to do this big move? Did I have the courage to do this? I felt sure I did. I knew that I was very excited and I knew that there wasn't much for my future in Amarillo. The worst part was yet to come though. Telling my grandmother was going to the hardest thing I ever had to do. Moving away from home, far away from home to strangers no less, let's just say it wasn't going to be a popular event. Even though my grandmother had four grandkids including me, she and I had something very special. We connected in many ways.

When I finally got my courage up, I told her about my plans. She cried and cried, it was truly horrible. I hope you understand that this is my Nana, the grandmother I talked about before. I don't want you to get the wrong impression of her, but she was a little self-centered to say the least. Her way of looking at things and people was how it or they were going to affect her and her life, it was all about her. When I was a child, I was to young to understand or see and that is the way it was for my sister and brothers. But as we grew up, we could see the way she truly was. I was the only one of the four of us who was close to her as an adult. I knew how to talk to her and I knew not to let the awful things she would sometimes say get to me and honestly I was the only one who would just tell her to shut up. Anyway I said to her don't you want me to happy after all it is my life. She just continued to cry and didn't say anything. It made me mad the way she was acting. She was acting like a spoiled child crying to get her way. I didn't say much else to her and didn't have or show any sympathy for her. You know what, as I sit here and write this, I remember that she and I never talked about it again, she never complained about my leaving her again and for her that is huge.

My father wasn't much better he didn't cry of course, but I knew that deep down he wasn't happy. He always used to say he wanted all of us kids to live in Amarillo just south of Western street. My Mom told me years later that he wasn't really unhappy, but just worried about what I was about to do and amazed at my courage.

I was amazed at my courage as well and wondered where in the world it came from. I think it came from the excitement I had and the passion I still have. Becoming a nanny, a really good nanny was very important to me. I knew that this was my chance. This was my future, I knew it with everything I had. I know now that Dad knew that too. He knew I had out grown little old Amarillo. Now though, bless his heart, no one not even Mom live in Amarillo. To Dad's credit though, he never said a word. I will forever love him for that. I believe that I now understand just how hard it was for him to let me go.

So the great pack up began, my mother and I got two large trunks and at least two big suitcases. I still have some pictures stashed away in some box somewhere of the family room with all of my stuff everywhere as I packed. I remember it was hard trying to decide what I needed and should bring and what could and should stay behind. Leaving my pets behind was very hard, at that time we had a little mixed breed dog named Midgie. She was what my father called, a little person in a dog suit. Midgie was extremely smart, almost to the point of being scary. I am ashamed to admit that no one in my family can take credit for her talents. She learned all that she knew all on her own. Midgie never weighted more than 5 pounds her whole seventeen years of life. The story of how we got her and her amazing talents could be a book all on its own. While I was packing I was wishing I could pack her to. It broke my heart to leave her and not be able to explain why. Saying goodbye to Midgie was a lot harder than saying goodbye to my family.

Finally the morning came, I was getting on a plane bound for New York. A whole world a way from simple little Amarillo. Saying goodbye to Mom and Dad and all was hard, but I knew if I fell all apart Dad would have never let me go. So I told myself not to look back and I got on that plane. In all the years I have been a nanny, I have had to say goodbye and give hugs a million times. It never gets easier, it is always hard at least for me. When I left for New York, families could say goodbye at the gate. While I was walking down the jet way, I was wondering to myself if I had just made the biggest mistake of my life. I have to admit I was scared but I knew I could get myself back home if I had to. When that plane took off, I said goodbye to my old life and I began to think of this as a wonderful adventure. A story that I could someday tell my grandkids about. The plane finally landed, I met the single mother and the struggle began.

CHAPTER TWO

NEW YORK

Live-in nannies are only required to commit to one year. This would turn out to be the longest year of my life. The boys were sweet and adorable, especially the youngest who was not yet two years old. The mother on the other hand was more interested in her social life than being a mother. I was on duty twenty four seven. Little did I know what lie ahead, about three weeks ahead to be exact. When I was just getting into a routine, the single mother landed in the hospital with a tumor in her uterus. I had the house, the kids and the car all to deal with on my own. Remember now this is my first real nanny position. Before this I had never been completely responsible for another family's house, car and kids for more than overnight. This would turn out to be for nearly four weeks. I had one saving grace however the single mother's parents lived next door and her mother was wonderful and soon became my best friend. I could have never made it all work without her. For almost four weeks I was the single mother. Every morning I had to get the boys up, dressed and fed and off to the bus stop on time for school and then deal with the baby all day. After school the boys and I did homework, lots of homework. We had dinner together and the boys took baths, we read stories and went to bed. I think I went to bed when the boys did. My days were very full with cooking, cleaning and the never ending laundry. The boys however were wonderful. I always enjoyed every minute I spent with them.

The single mother got out of the hospital not long before Thanksgiving. I knew the holidays would be hard. I had never been away from home during the holiday season. Thanksgiving wasn't so bad, everyone in the country celebrates it mostly in the same way. Its all about the food and football, right? Although I did learn something during that Thanksgiving, my Mom makes the best stuffing or as she calls it dressing in the world. I missed that very much. I knew Christmas would be much worse. I was already incredibly homesick. It hit me really hard when I got my presents in the mail from home. I remember when my presents came, I opened the box and inside were several wrapped gifts. As I lifted them out one at a time to put under the tree, I began to cry. Then without really thinking about it, I carefully opened one of the presents. I looked at it through all the tears in my eyes, I think it was a watch and then I carefully rewrapped it and put it with the rest under the tree. It made me feel better at least for a moment. The feeling didn't last, it was terrible, all I wanted to do is cry and go home. I would talk to my family on the phone about once a week. Usually talking to Mom especially would make me feel better, but during Christmas, it only made me feel more miserable and homesick. The boys helped some because nothing makes Christmas fun like little kids. I didn't want to ruin things for them, so I buried my sadness deep inside and played the role of a happy nanny. I was never so happy to see the end of the holiday season as I was that year. When it ended I grew less homesick and we went back to somewhat normal routine.

In February the single mother began talking about all of us taking a trip to Texas on the train. Through me talking about them constantly and many phone conversations, the single mother had developed a relationship with my family. She decided she wanted to meet them face to face. This was great news to me, but I knew very well not to get my hopes up to high. I also knew that things might not go well at all when we got to Texas. I was worried about my father and the single mother getting along together. I knew that my father would not like the way the single mother at times treated her children. She was at times pretty harsh with them. My father was not one to keep his feelings to himself, especially not in his own home. I was afraid that we wouldn't be able to stay together in the house. I decided to keep my feelings to myself and hope for the best or as my Mom always says we will cross that bridge when we get to it. I didn't tell Mom and Dad about the possible visit either, no sense in making them all depressed when it doesn't work out. That is exactly what I thought, that this trip was one of the single mother's pipe dreams and it wouldn't happen.

As time grew closer though, the single mother began making serious plans. This trip really was going to happen, I couldn't believe it. Just when I was always getting super frustrated with her and about to explode, she would do something that would make everything all right. I don't know about you, but people like that drive me nuts. This trip was to take place during the kids spring break from school. When she finally bought train tickets for the trip, I told my family of the plans to come and visit, needless to say they were happy and excited. Just before all of this the single mother had started a new job. She didn't seem to think that they might not like the idea of her taking vacation so soon. She also decided not to tell her mother about the trip until the night before we were to leave. I really can't for the life of me understand where in the world this woman's head was at, do you? Who asked for vacation time right after they started a new job, that alone is nuts. But the one I really can't wrap my head around is not telling her mother. I know some of you are thinking what is so crazy about that. I just can't image it, my mother and I are extremely close I tell her everything. I don't understand why she didn't her mother, maybe she was afraid of what her mother might say or do I guess.

Everything was coming together quickly, everyone at both ends were very excited. The boys were asking me all sorts of questions about my family, the house, dogs and cats and all. It took my parents and I forever to make the single mother understand that Raton New Mexico is closer to Amarillo than Dallas is. The train doesn't go to Amarillo and the closest two stops are either Raton or Dallas. The single mother just couldn't understand how a place in a different state is closer to where we were going than one in the same state, it just didn't any sense to her. It always amazes me how people didn't pay any attention in elementary geography class. It is a five to six hour drive from Dallas to Amarillo and only a three to four hour drive from Raton to Amarillo. My parents were going to meet the train in Raton and drives us back to Amarillo.

Anyway the day before departure, the single mother calls me from work. She tells me that her new boss didn't approve her vacation plans. Duh, I still can't believe she actually thought they would. She says to me that she can't go. I fully expected her next statement to be that the trip was cancelled. Boy, was I surprised and shocked when she asked me if I wanted to take the older two boys and go. She said the toddler would stay home with her and either her mother and this friend of her's would care for him while she was working. In the seconds after she said that I thought to myself, okay here comes the biggest challenge of your life if you say yes. I said yes of course and we hung up. I spent the rest of the afternoon thinking about it. I thought about the fact that her mother had really bad knees and really wasn't able to care for an active and big toddler anymore and frankly she shouldn't have to either. Then there was the matter of this friend of the single mother. She was not an option at all. Why you ask, because she had two kids of her own that she didn't take care of and her house was extremely dirty and that is being nice. There were dirty clothes thrown around everywhere and dirty dishes all over. There was even a mouse nest in one of her living room chairs. What totally blew my mind about that was that she knew about the mouse nest and wasn't planning on doing anything about it. Okay, ready, one, two, three, Gross! I wouldn't leave my goldfish with this woman for thirty minutes much less a small child. So when the single mother came home, I told her that we needed to talk and I took her in my room and shut the door. I told her what I had been thinking about all afternoon. I said that I wanted to take the toddler with me. I took a deep breathe and prayed that she wouldn't get mad and yell at me. At that moment I remembered all those times when my mother tried with everything she had to teach me tact. As you can plainly see that is a lesson I have not yet mastered. To my amazement, the single mother didn't get mad or yell, she agreed with me. I was not a witness to the single mother telling her mother that night about the plans. That night I don't think I slept more than two minutes all night. I spent the night thinking about what I had just gotten myself into and how in the world I was going to handle it all. I was also a little mad at myself, I thought okay idiot you have really gone and opened your big mouth this time and now you have a ton of possible problems. The next morning me, three boys, three suitcases and a stroller got on the train.

I need to explain one thing about this trip. This job caring for these boys started in November and this trip took place in March. Now I ask you, would you allow someone you had known only such a short time to take your children half way across the country alone on the train? I don't think most people would have even considered it. This single mother did't have a problem with it. One of my friends said that she thought it was a compliment to me, the single mother trusted me and knew I could handle it and the boys were in the best possible care. The way I look at it is, she got a vacation from her kids and that is what she wanted and why she didn't argue with me about taking the toddler.

We got on the train and to my amazement the toddler didn't cry when the single mother left us on the train. We had a room if you want to call it that. I think my term for it would have been large walk in closet. It really was the size of a large and I use that term loosely walk in closet. It had two bunk beds that folded down from one wall and there was a very tiny bathroom, like the ones on airplanes, expect this one had a shower I think. The boys were very excited as we watched the train pull out from our window. The toddler was saying choo choo, so cute. Also let me say that you would be very hard pressed to find boys who behaved better than those boys did on that trip. They were angles the entire trip. We spent about thirty six hours on a train. The first night was easy, we went to the dinning car for dinner. The boys thought it was very cool to be sitting in a moving dinning room. We talked about all we saw of the window as we ate dinner. After dinner we explored the train. The boys were being little kids, laughing and playing and running a little through the train. I knew that they were most likely bothering some people, but you know what I didn't care. Kids have to be allowed to be kids. They can't be perfect little angels all the time, besides I think the best and most beautiful noise in the world is the sound of a child's laughter. So I just ignored all the looks I got from all the old prunes on that train and let my boys have some fun before bedtime. Don't get me wrong, I wasn't letting the boys scream and yell or open other people's doors. They were just being happy kids, just playing and having fun, not being mean little brats. There was a method to this madness, the boys had to run off steam before going to bed anyway. This is before games boys and play stations and all of that, the sights out of a window are only entertaining for just so long especially for boys. I had to find ways of to entertain them.

Sleeping was going to be interesting as well. Two twin sized bunk beds, four people, do you see the problem? I set up the older boys on the upper bunk, a head at each end. The toddler and I slept on the bottom bunk. Again for the second night in a row I don't think I slept more than two minutes all night long. Sleeping with a toddler on a full sized bed is difficult, sleeping with a toddler on a twin sized bed is impossible. I put him on the inside close to the wall so he couldn't fall off. He was excited and didn't want to sleep, so it took him a while to settle down. I read a story to all three of them and they all were out like lights. All night I was always moving some part of his little body off or out of the middle of me. Besides that the train was moving and stopping all night long.

The next morning I was exhausted after out first night on the train. We went to the dinning car for breakfast and the boys ate enough pancakes to fill up a elephant. It was fun watching them enjoy, but a mess, the toddler had syrup from head to toe I think. By this point I was really regretting my decision to do this crazy train trip, even though I was going to see my family. I put on a happy face for the boys and told myself that I was stuck so buck up and deal with it. Later that morning we arrived in Chicago. The Chicago train station is really something to see, it is huge and very beautiful. There is wood work everywhere and all the floors are marble. We had to change trains there, we had about a three hour layover. I had the boys pile the suitcases on the stroller and told them to push it and I carried the toddler. That was the best nearly three hours of the trip on the train, because the Chicago train station has a big playground right in the middle of it and it also has some of the best hot dogs I have ever had. So we had a great hot dog for lunch and the boys got a chance to run and play on this very cool playground. We found the train that we needed to be on and got settled in for another night on the train. That layover in Chicago did wonders for my morale, because I got through the first night on the train and managed to get through the Chicago train station without missing the train or losing a child. I slept better the second night only because I think I was completely exhausted. I probably could have slept through almost anything including sleeping with a toddler. The next morning the boys were excited as we went to breakfast, they were almost there. Lunch came and shortly after we arrived in LaJunta Colorado. I don't know if you have ever been in the city of LaJunta or not but its about the size of a big city mall. The train stopped as it did in all the little towns along the way. Some people got off and some people actually got on. I say that because you must understand by this point, I was just about to go completely nuts. I was locked in a large walk-in closet with a window and three kids. No radio, television or anything for entertainment except what was going by outside the window. Plus that there was this never ending stream of questions about everything from dirt to space, but the most popular one was when are we going to be there. That train trip was a real test of my patience and skills with little kids. Just as I was beginning to wonder why we were still sitting in LaJunta. They announced over the loud speaker in the train that there was a derailed freight train a few miles up the track. They said that they were going to wait for a while and see if they could clear the track. They told us to feel free to get off the train and wander around the town, but not to go to far. They would blow the train whistle when we were ready to leave. There was a park across the street, so the boys and I went over there to play for what turned out to be an hour and a half. I actually didn't mind this delay at this point, it was nice being outside, out of the walk in closet and the boys were having fun running around. When they finally did blow the train whistle, I thought okay great, now I am ready to finish this train trip. But my excitement didn't last very long. As we got back on the train, the loud speaker was saying that we couldn't wait any longer for them to fix the derailed freight train. We have connections to make in Albuquerque they said. This train's final destination was California. They told us to collect all of our personal belongs and get off the train. They were putting all of us on buses bound for Albuquerque. After a few brief moments of total panic, I took a deep breath and told myself to pull yourself together, you have to take care of the boys. I didn't know exactly what to do at that point, I was scared to death and I think the older boys knew something was wrong. I knew for sure I didn't want to go all the way to Albuquerque. My parents were just an hour and a half or so up the track in Raton.

In the meantime, my parent had been sitting in an empty Raton train station for at least two hours. The single mother back in New York was calling the eight hundred number to find out about the train and she was hearing only one word "derailment". So she was thinking that her nanny and three sons are on a derailed train. I think at one point my parents called the single mother in New York from a pay phone to try to find out what was happening with the train. I know this sounds like it should be coming out of some novel about kidnapping and the feds and such, but believe it or not it is all true. I was feeling completely helpless and cutoff from the world. I would have given anything for a cell phone that day. This story wouldn't be quite as good I don't think if I had been able to call Mom and the single mother in New York. Now that I think about it, Mom's cell phone is buried in the bottom of her purse and she can't hear ringing or it is turned off or worse yet, she doesn't even have it with her. So a cell phone most likely would not have been much help after all.

While the boys and I were standing there waiting for instructions or an Amtrax man that I could talk to. I was feeling completely helpless and alone, I could't communicate with the single mother in New York or with my parents. Talk about wanting to pull your hair out, OMG! Then I saw an Amtrax man and I quickly went over and told him my sad story. I asked him if I could call the Raton station, my parents are there. He said no that station is closed down, no one is there. While all of this was going on, my poor Dad was driving up the road to see if he could see the train coming. The Amtrax man told of us with issues to wait a minute and he went over and had a meeting with several other Amtrax men. I felt sorry for those guys, everyone was yelling and complaining at them and none of this was fault. After several more minutes of panic and trying to keep the boys together and happy, the older boys were asking what was happening and why and all those curious kid questions. The train man came back and told all of us with issues that there would be five buses that go non-stop to Albuquerque and one bus that goes to Albuquerque but stops at all the little places in-between like Raton. Right there and then I looked up at the sky and said thank you to the good Lord. I told the boys to come with me over to the bus making all the stops in between. The bus was very full and hot. The boys were hungry, hot and tried. Anyone who has children or who has worked with children, knows that this is a very bad combination. The bus took off with the toddler on my lap and the older boys in seats behind me. Two very long hours later, the bus pulled into the empty Raton train station, the door opened and there stood Mom and Dad. I was never so happy to see them as I was that day. They were surprised to see the toddler, I called Mom and Dad before I talked to the single mother about bringing the toddler with me, so they thought he wasn't coming. After a quick diaper change and a brief stop at McDonald's to feed my hungry boys, we were on the road towards Amarillo. It took us about three and a half hours to get to Amarillo. The boys just couldn't wait to get there. The middle boy, who was six years old at the time, must have asked my father about a hundred times, are we there yet? The boys tested my Dad's patience too.

One of the funniest things happened when we finally got to my parent's house. The boys followed me into my bedroom and that time I had a waterbed. I guess the boys had never seen or been on a waterbed, because their reaction when they crawled up on it was so funny. The two older boys stopped moving instantly and just froze and said whats wrong with your bed, its lumpy and it moves! I told them it was a waterbed, they were amazed and had loads of fun playing on it. I didn't say no to the boys much on this trip, I pretty much let them do whatever they wanted within reason. They didn't get to have much fun on a normal basis, their parents fought a lot and they didn't see their Dad all that much either. So this trip was all about their happiness and letting them have some much needed fun.

All of my family fell head over heels in love with the boys. The sad part of this story is that none of the boys ever asked for their mother or even to talk to her on the phone. At that time the boys were only eight, six and twenty-two months old. The older boys loved my older brother and had more fun hanging out with him. He taught them how to play poker and they thought he was the coolest dude on the planet, which by the way did wonders for my older brother's ego. I remember one afternoon my brother and I took the boys bowling. The toddler started to try to run up the alley after the bowling ball, saying ball, ball. I remember we laughed so hard, my brother still talks about that day and what fun we had. My family and I also took the boys to Wonderland Park, it is an amusement park. The toddler loved the merry-go-round, "horsey, horsey" he would say. My grandmother thought he was the cutest ever put on the face of this earth. We did everything there was to do in Amarillo. The boys had a blast but the day came to get back on the train and go back to New York. The older boys didn't want to go and were crying when we got back on the train. I told them not to be sad that someday we all could go back again, knowing full well that wasn't true. I didn't want to go back either, but I couldn't let them know that. I told them about all the fun things that they get to tell their mother about and their friends in school. That seemed to help the mood some. The trip back to New York was uneventful, which is a blessing, I am not sure I could have handled any problems. When we got back, the single mother was right there to meet us, I think whether she wanted to admit it or not, she missed her boys very much. The boys were very happy to see her too. She heard every detail of the trip in gross detail in car ride from the station to the house. The boys made books for school apt their trip to Texas on the train and all the things they got to see and do.

After that trip the rest of the year just seemed to fly by. I had to deal with the single mother and her lack of time for her kids and with the fights she would have with their father on the phone. I am ashamed to admit but once they were screaming at each other on the phone and I took the phone from her hand and hung it up. As you can image she got mad and yelled at me and I told her that I was just done listening to it and she could be mad if she wanted to I didn't care. I walked away and she didn't say anything else, I think that deep down she was glad I did it and thought it was kind of funny. When my birthday rolled around in October, she asked me what I wanted. I told her that all I wanted was an entire weekend off, from Friday evening until Monday morning. She said okay, but I never did get my entire weekend off. I worked twenty hours a day that entire year.

When November came, my year was done and I decided to go home. The single mother asked me to stay several times, but I told her that I just couldn't live her lifestyle anymore. It was hard saying goodbye to the boys, because I didn't know what was going to happen to them. But I had to go and take care of me, so I did. I had to take the bus all the way back, New York city to Amarillo Texas. The trip wasn't all that bad. Having an Ipod on that trip would have just about made it perfect, the only problem, no ipods in 1990. Anyway you would be amazed at the interesting people you meet and places you see while riding the bus halfway across the country. The bus trip home could be another book all on its own, needless to say I made it home safe and sound. That was a tough year, it made me grow up quickly and take responsibility for things and people that I never had to before. That year in New York with that single mother helped me more than any nanny training class could ever in learning communication, trust, honesty, patience, endurance and love, especially love.

CHAPTER THREE

NANNY ISSUES

After I got home it was the holiday season again. The nanny agency was already after me to sign on again with another family. I told them that I wasn't doing anything until after the holidays. I was very excited about Christmas and getting to be with my family. It was great to be able to live a lifestyle that I liked and I was used to. That is the hardest part about a live-in nanny, living under some else's roof and living their lifestyle. There is no way you can truly understand how difficult it is until you try it. I have had people say, oh I know how you feel, I lived with my mother or something like that. Relatives don't count, because you know each other, you came from the same planet or cut from the same block if you know what I mean. When you are a live-in nanny you are expected to move in with strangers, that is what they start as strangers. I mean you have met at least one face to face interview and a few phone conversations, but you really know each other well. One would hope that you would soon become friends and if you are like me, extended family members, most of them anyway. As a live-in nanny, you learn after so many years to live in one room. I am here to tell you that old habits die real hard. I was a live-out nanny for a while and I shared a house with a friend who is also a live out nanny. Just like I have for years I still lived in my room and not in the rest of the house. My friend used to tease me about it, she would say, you can live in the rest of the house you know, you are not a live-in nanny anymore. I guess once a live-in nanny always a live in. Over the years I have become very comfortable with my part of the house just being my room and it was very hard to change that. It was hard to let the world extend outside of my room. Now I am living with my Mom and older brother and that problem doesn't exist.

I have some friends that are nannies and they have had a terrible time adjusting to life under someone else's roof. One friend really had a terrible time, almost everything that the parents did drove her crazy. She would get mad at me because I didn't always take her side in every situation. At those times, I would just remind her of what is very true, it is their house and their children, they can do whatever they want. No matter how many times I said that to her, she never seemed to be able to not let the things the parents did drive her so crazy. I guess I am lucky in the fact that I could go into my room and close the door and the entire world goes away. The only world that did exist was within the four walls of my room. In my room I was surrounded by pictures of my family and other important treasures of mine. When I would go into my room, it was like going home everyday. I had always worked hard at keeping it that way. It always bugs me when someone complains about trying to cram everything they own into a three bedroom condo or something. I wish, I always think to myself, you need to trade places with me for a while then we will talk. People who are career live-in nannies are very portable people. I used to have a rule of thumb in regards to stuff, it had to fit in the pickup I had at the time. If I didn't buy so much it would not fit in the truck. That way I would save money as well, because someday moving was going to happen. I used to be able to fit everything I owned in two large trunks, two or three suitcases and maybe a box or two. I can tell you that those days are over. It really messes things up when you start buying furniture. Also it seems like the older you become, the more junk you just can't live without, oh well.

In all my years as a live-in nanny I have learned to treasure the space in the house that did belong to me. I have never allowed any maids that the family might have to clean my room. I have never liked that even as a kid and my Mom had someone clean the house. Usually this person Mom had to clean was someone I knew well and cared about as well. I just didn't like the idea of anyone bothering my stuff. My room is the only place in the house that belongs to me and it had always been my safe haven. Even now living with Mom and my older brother, I still feel like my room is my space. I keep the door closed most of the time. As a live-in nanny my room was the only place where I could go and almost be at home. When I say almost at home, I don't mean that I have never felt at home or welcome in the homes I have lived in because I have very much so. What I mean is home with my family, with pictures and special stuff all around the room, it is like being home. I guess I have always felt that anyone who invaded that space was trespassing where they didn't belong. Please don't misunderstand me, I always allowed my kids and the the parents thereof in my room. All of my kids loved hanging out in Carol's room. It was important to me to keep those two worlds separate, the family that I cared for and my own family's world. I think if I were to let those two worlds come completely together, my room wouldn't have feel so much like going home anymore. Live-in nannies who can keep those worlds separate, find life easier because their room does turn into a safe haven, like going home.

There is the issue of privacy, it is a huge problem at times for a live-in nanny. As a live-in nanny you have to protect your privacy and not invade the parent's privacy either. First time parents struggle with this because they worry about more than the nanny does. All of this is new to them and like dealing with a nervous first time mother, a nanny must deal with the parents concerns with kid gloves. I had a friend who was a live out nanny, but then moved to France to be a live-in nanny. She got a quick crash course on what my life was like. I hope she adjusted to it all well.

Traveling with the family that you care for is not always easy or fun, because it is their vacation not yours. You sometimes feel like a third wheel or like you don't really belong there. One family I worked with for a short time took me on one of their skiing vacations. We stayed at one their friend's homes. I had to stay upstairs in my two rooms of the house. I was allowed to go down to the kitchen to get my meals and than return to my rooms upstairs. I could come down and go outside or whatever on my time off duty, but I wasn't allowed to hang out in the family room with them at all. They worked very hard at making sure I was not included. I was just an employee or I think a second class citizen to them. That was definitely not one of those fun times traveling with a family. I felt very lonely and sad and I don't want to say that I hated the parents, because I don't think that was really true. I must admit that trip and their treatment of me did not help our relationship. Most of my families that I have traveled with didn't do that, they always worked hard at making sure I was included and I was having fun as well. I have always struggled with even when I was traveling with the best families not feeling left out while they go off to do something fun, while I had to stay in the hotel or whatever while the baby naps or something. As a nanny especially a live in nanny, you have to maintain some level of distance so things like that don't hurt you, because the family is not really trying to hurt you, they are just trying to enjoy their vacation. Which you as their nanny are getting to go for free, remembering that is not always easy when you are left in the hotel room with a screaming baby and they are going to hang out on the beach.

Hours, where do I start? Everyone who has ever had a job of any kind struggles with hours, either there are to many hours or not enough hours. Most of the positions I had I worked about twelve hours a day and I think that was about the normal for most nannies. There will be families who want different hours, like weekend time. I have always felt that weekend time was mine and I didn't want to work then, except for the occasional babysitting. But then I started thinking about what I think a nanny should be ready to do for a family. What I mean is the nanny job is not about talking care of just the children, it's about caring for the family. When you care for a family where the parents work long hours and the only time they have alone together is in bed at night. The best thing for the children is to have mom and dad together and loving each other and happy. As nanny you have to sometimes help take care of the marriage, by willing to work weekends. This is a two way street however, the parents have to be able to give you a day off during the week if they have working on the weekends.

I know that there are some parents who will abuse this, this is where communication comes, talk about it and come to an agreement on hours, that you both stick too.

A position I had, the parents requested weekend time from me, they were able to give a day or two during the week. I was always proud of the fact that I was always very flexible and willing to work with people. They had another nanny that worked on Saturdays and she was asking for more hours. The parents didn't want to lose her, so they came to me and asked if I was willing to share hours with her. I appreciated the fact the parents asked me if I willing, they didn't just demand that I share hours with the other nanny, which they could have done. The parents also allowed the other nanny and I to decide which one of us worked when, we were in charge of the schedule. I was willing to share with her because I liked her very much and because of the way the parents were handling it. So the other nanny and I worked out the hours and who worked when and a started date for this new schedule was set. Have you ever said you would do something and than later regret it. One of the days I was going to work was on Sundays when the new schedule started. I was so mad at myself in the days before the schedule started, wishing that I had never agreed to it.

It was until a few months later that I learned just how important the other nanny was to me. The mother got very ill and was in the hospital for about a month. I could have never been able to handle all that was handed to me without her. This family also taught me something that I don't think they ever intended to. A live in nanny needs to be careful and not let families take advantage of her. While the mother was in the hospital I was working all the time, day and night. I was okay with that, I knew it was what I had to do to help this father. But after she got better and came home, they expected the very long hours to continue, they wanted nanny care twenty-four hours a day, seven days a week. The nanny I shared time with had another job and a husband and couldn't work but maybe three days a week, all of the rest of the time was mine. I tried talking to the parents about it and they were not willing to change anything. The only thing I could do to change the situation was leave and I did. I guess what I am trying to say is don't let families take advantage of you. Help out as much as you can when the situation calls for it, but make sure things go back to normal. On the day I left that house and family I felt like I was escaping from jail.

CHAPTER FOUR

FAMILIES, KIDS & LOVE

Families are all different. Until I became a nanny and saw other families close up, I thought my family was a normal American family. I learned that my family is not the norm at all. In my childhood home there was no fighting, no words said in anger, there was just love. As a nanny, I saw that most homes are not like mine, that there is some fighting and words said that shouldn't have been said. Families have tested my ability to make the world go away by closing the door of my room. A marriage was falling completely apart, there were loud fights and some of those happened in front of the kids. The tension in the house would get so thick you would probably need a steak knife to cut it. I remember trying to make things as happy and stress free during the day for the kids while the parents were at work. Here is a lesson that was a very hard for me to learn. Actually I am not sure I ever really did learn it completely. As a nanny you can't let your feelings for the children interfere with what is the best for you. When the parents would fight, I always had a terrible time dealing with it. My mother knows this all too well, because I would call her, usually in tears. If the life you have with the family is rough and not working out for you. Then take my advice and get out. There is only person that you truly have to take care of and that is you. One of my biggest issues is always putting my kids first. I always put the needs of the kids I take care of first before my own needs. I just can't help it, that is what I do. A nanny needs to remember that the kids have parents and family, they will be okay. I guess I need to practice what I preach, huh! You need to think about what is best for you first, not the kids. Especially when you come across a family with a bad track record. Nanny agencies will not usually warn you, because for them it is about the money. If you meet a family, who has had problems keeping a nanny, first ask yourself why, it could be money, it could be hours or living conditions. There are tons of reasons why they have problems, you may not be able to find the real reason. A nanny needs to learn that it will most likely never work out and it is wrong to think that you can fix their issues. The reason is simple and something you probably learned in elementary school, people are who they are and you can't change them into something they are not. Whatever the problem the family has keeping a nanny is the family's problem and they are the only ones who can solve it. It is hard though I know because the ones who suffer are the children. Little children invest most of themselves in the people that they love. When a family has issues with keeping a nanny and is getting a new one all the time. The rules change and the kids to let go of the last nanny and attach to the new one. If you as a nanny have to leave a family for whatever reason, it's hardest on the kids, but it's hard on you as the nanny as well, because whether you want to or not, you get attached to the little ones. The little faces, smiles, giggles and the endless stream of love that is addicting. Speaking of love that is one of the bees things about being a nanny, the strong bonds you build with the children. The kids spend most of the day during the week with you for years at a time in most cases. The kids learn to you and you fall in love with them. Sometimes those attachments can cause problems. I have had two situations where the mother could have some issues with bonds between me and their children. In the first family, the mother was very accepting of it. She understood that her child loved me and I loved him and that he was in the best possible care when he was with me. She would come home in time for bed time. This little guy was about a your old at the time. Anyway she wanted to hold and rock and read to him. He would scream and cry and run after me when I would leave the room. She would just smile and laugh and kiss him goodnight and say thanks to me. I always respected her a fret deal for that. I am not sure that if it were my child wanting to be with someone else instead of with me, that I could be so accepting and understanding. This is where communication comes into play big time. You as a nanny must work on your relationship with the parents as hard as you work on your relationship with the kids. You have to able to talk and be honest with each other. With communication and honestly you will both learn to trust and respect each other. Another one of my little boys had a very close bond with me and would tell people that he and I were going to get married when he was a very little boy. He was so cute because he would tell people that he was going to wear a top hat and tails to our wedding. I tell you what there is nothing else that makes me feel better than that. He loved me with all of his little heart. This mother also handled it well, we talked about it a lot and she thought it was funny and very sweet. I am totally addicted to is the never ending unconditional love you always get from the kids. Not to mention those little faces, smile, eyes, giggles and hugs and kisses form the kids. Through good times and bad, you are there for the kids and they are there for you. I was a live out nanny for this wonderful family. They have twin girls who were seven months old when I started and were nearly three when I left. I must admit that there were times that I wished that I would have just packed up my stuff and left after my last live in position ended and never gotten involved with this family, but then I would walk in their front door and those adorable little faces would be smiling at me. I would go in and sit down and they would climb on my lap. One of them likes to get close and look at you, eye to eye and say hi. That little face with those big amazing blue eyes, looking at me with nothing but unconditional love. I ask you how could anyone want to leave leave that? I was stuck between a rock and a hard place. There was the side that wanted to move away, anywhere really, the destination really didn't matter. Then there was the part that was in love with these two little girls with the amazing blue eyes. For a while I didn't have an answer, then I started homeschooling the girls a little with this program the mother brought. I discovered the solution to my problem, the girls are very smart and quickly showed me that they needed more, they needed to be in school. So I talked to the parents and the girls started school full time and I left. I am very happy to tell you that they are doing very well and are very happy.

As a nanny and now I have always kind of lived life one day at a time or one week at a time. Women are saying oh I am becoming so much like my mother, well I guess I am becoming more like my mother. Because she is always saying something that fits perfectly here and that is we will cross that bridge when we get to it. In other words worry about tomorrow when tomorrow comes. Good old mom, you can never go wrong quoting her. I can't leave the Dad out of this, he motto was "Calmness in the face of adversity is a great asset." He lived by that all of his life and I can still hear him saying it to me.

CHAPTER FIVE

VIRGINIA

After the holidays ended, I started talking to the agencies again. This time the location was the DC area. This agency had me fly in and interview with the families in person. This was a change for the better. I will never again take a job with only a phone conversation for an interview.

I will remember that flight into DC all of my life. It was January and very cold. There had been a bad ice storm, the airport had lost power completely. So the jet ways were not working and they had us walk out of the back of the plane down to the ground and into the airport. There was a very tall man on the flight. I am talking really tall man and when we walked out of the plane, we had to walk under the wing of the plane. You are beginning to get the picture, right? He forgot or didn't think he needed to duck. He hit his head on the wing of the plane and fell over backwards like a dead tree. The sound he made and the sound his head made when it hit the wing of that plane is something I will never forget. The airport people attended to him and the rest of us walked into the building, trying very hard not to laugh out loud, not laughing to yourself was impossible. I am sorry that was funny. Then they began to bring our luggage in one piece at a time. I am not kidding, one at a time. I have little sympathy for people when they complain about slow baggage service at the airport after that experience.

I spent the next three days staying with the head of the nanny agency while I interviewed with families. She lived in Foggy Bottom, which is a neighborhood in DC. It is old and wonderful and for a small town girl who loves history and old things it was heaven.

Carol Kelly

First impressions are always interesting. I will never forget the first meeting I had with the mother who would soon become a huge part of my life. She picked me up at the metro station. She was then and is now a beautiful lady, bright and outgoing. I catch myself feeling uneasy around ladies like that, like I am not good enough. I try not to and wish I could stop feeling that way. Even though we are very different, something just told me that she and I could work. I have to admit my first impression of her was that she was a bit of an airhead. That first impression could not have been more wrong. The family lived in a large house in Virginia. They had two little boys, one that was two and a half and one that was about three months old. The father and I hit it off and he and I could joke around from the start. We both have strange sense of humor. Their house was by far the largest I had ever lived in at that time. My room was in the basement, a very big basement. It had a door that led out to the pool in the backyard. My room was big, four poster bed, the works. I used to make jokes with my family about the little tiny bathroom I had in that basement. You know what is funny about that house with the pool. I am a good swimmer and love to swim, but I only remember getting into that pool maybe once or twice the entire time we lived in that house. The family moved while I was working for them, not far away, smaller house, no pool. The pool made the mother very nervous, she worried about the boys constantly. Don't get me wrong I totally agree, those things happen so very fast.

I started in January, the mother and I did real well together and always had lots of laughs. The baby spent most of his time on my hip.

One Saturday I came home, I had been out with friends shopping. Anyway I came home and the Dad was there with the boys. The two year old was crying and very unhappy. The Dad came to me and says please help, he is very unhappy and mad at me and I don't know what he wants. I went to the two year old and knelt down. His little face had big tears on his cheeks. I asked him what was wrong. He said "Carol, I want to watch under the sea and have some toothpaste cookies". Under the sea was he called the Disney movie "The Little Mermaid" and toothpaste cookies is the name he gave Girl Scout thin mint cookies. I explained to the father what he wanted and a couple minutes later, the two year old was happily sitting in his little chair watching his movie and eating his cookies. By the way I think his name for Girl Scout thin mint cookies

24

is perfect, they do taste like toothpaste covered in chocolate. I like Girls Scout cookies but I don't like the thin mints.

One of the best part of those two years was the friends I made. Those bonds still exists today. The best one of those friends was a nanny who lived just across this huge park. She lived with a nice family with one baby girl who was the same age as my little one. We met at a nanny CPR training class. This class was arranged by the agency that had placed both of us and they introduced us because they knew we lived close together and we were close to the same age. From the start it was like being reunited with an old friend. The connection between us was instant. Soon we were together nearly every day if we not we were talking on the phone. We did things with the kids, playgrounds, the zoo etc. One of our favorite things was going out to eat breakfast at this restaurant. They had a buffet with everything you could possibly imagine for breakfast. The kids always got a hearty breakfast on those mornings. I remember they always had these little white powder donuts. I bet our three kids ate more that a thousand of those donuts. My oldest boy would ask me everyday if we were going to get those little donuts today or not. He really didn't care about all the other foods on the buffet, just the donuts.

Her room was in the basement of their home as well. That basement and that house became like a second home to me. We spent weekends together, mainly going shopping and hanging out with her parents and family. She grew up in the area. When we first met she couldn't drive a car. I taught her to drive, it took time and a ton of patience and encouragement but she finally learned to do it and well I might add. We also spent a ton of time hanging out with the family she worked for. One of my favorite memories is one weekend the parents invited us to have dinner with them. The mother had spent all day that day baking this big squash. She had decided to make her own baby food. My friend their nanny and I and the father as well were kind of grossed out by the idea of making the baby girl eat that squash. It really didn't look good at all. Well, it didn't matter what any of us said about it. The mother put in the blender and then at dinner fed it to the baby girl. The face the baby made was priceless. We all laughed and laughed, I am not sure if they ever fed her any more of that squash or not. Another memory that she and I were just talking about not long ago that happened in that basement, we went to rent a movie and got some snacks and had come back to watch the movie. We had settled down to watch the movie, she got some nachos and a diet cherry coke and I don't remember exactly what I got for snack. Anyway before long the combination of coke and nachos began to have a very funny affect. She began burping, I am talking major burps. We got the giggles big time and they just got worse with every single burp. I think we laughed and laughed for almost two hours that night. I don't think we watched much of the movie we rented, we were laughing too hard. The next morning the father asked us what in the world was so funny, he had heard us laughing. I still chuckle to this day when I think about it. In fact when she and I were talking about it not long ago, we were both laughing.

That first summer the family I worked for took me with them on their vacation to the beach. I am not much of a beach person, mainly because I have red hair and I usually end up getting bright red like a lobster. They rented a house on the Outer Banks of North Carolina, they loved it. It was great, very beautiful and there were wild horses. I think it was that first summer, we were loading the car and because of the car seats I was going to have to ride in the very back behind the back seat where usually the suitcases would go. So the suitcases had to be put on top of the care in the luggage rack. If I remember correctly it was raining on the way down. We made an attempt to cover the suitcases with a large tarp, but it wasn't working well and we had to stop several times on the road.

When we finally got there, I remember walking on the beach with the three year old one day. He stopped and looked out on the ocean and just stood there for a few minutes. I asked him what he was thinking about. He looked at me and said do you think there are people on the beach over there looking this way, pointing with his little finger towards the water. I said you mean on the other side of the ocean and he said yeah. I told him probably, but they can't see us just like we can't see them. This kid had just turned three a few weeks prior, that is amazing thought for someone that was only three I think. A day or so later, the neighbors down the road left their garage door open and some wild horses decided to make themselves at home in there. One of them came over and asked if we knew what to do or if we could help. I said I could get the horses out for them. I went over, everyone around was standing outside watching the horses in the garage. I told everyone to move away so that the horses would have room to run. I found a large stick on the ground and walked carefully in. Horses are strange animals, if you act like you are afraid of them, they will take advantage, but if you act like you are the boss and know what you are doing they will respect you. As I walked in slowly, the horses all crowed to one side of the garage. I walked to the back and hit the stick hard on the garage floor and yelled loud, the horses quickly ran out of the garage and away. The neighbors were grateful and my family was impressed and I felt really good. We stayed there for a week, it was always loads of fun and I will always be grateful that they wanted to include me.

I ended up having to spend another Christmas away from home and family that year. This time however I was not nearly as homesick as I was before. I think the reason was this family was intact and the house was full of love. That love didn't exist in the single mother's home.

Oh my gosh, I am leaving out an important character in this family's story. They had a dog, just your average mutt. He was black and brown and he was about knee high. He was sweet in his own way, but he was jealous of the boys and my personal opinion of him was that he was as dumb as a post.

One of his favorite tricks was to take one of the kid's toys and go under the coffee table and growl. My nickname for him soon became the "wonder idiot." The mother didn't care much for my nickname for the dog and would always give me a slightly dirty looks when I called him that. I think she knew down deep that my nickname was the perfect for him and I figure if the shoe fits, you know.

When the baby was about ten months old, the family moved to a smaller house without a pool. It was only a few blocks away from the old house. My room was still in the basement, smaller room but still nice.

The funniest thing happened one day while we lived in that house. There was a deck in the backyard, this deck was not raised off the ground like most, it sat on the ground. At one of the outside corners of the deck by the steps down to the grass, there was a small hole in the lattice work around the bottom of the deck. Where a small animal or a dumb dog could go under the deck, the space was very tight under there. So one day I had just put the boys down for a nap and I had come downstairs for what I hoped was about an hour of peace and quiet. The dog was outside in the backyard. I had just sat down to relax when all a sudden I heard this awful noise coming from the backyard, I opened the back sliding glass door and step out on the deck. I realized two things, one was that the sound was coming from under the deck and two was that there two noises and one was the dumb dog and the other sound I could not identify for sure. I quickly went back inside and got a hammer and a screw driver from the kitchen drawer. You know the drawer I am talking about every kitchen in every household in America has one. It has everything in it from band aids to tools. I used the hammer and screw driver to pry up the two lose boards on the deck. Yes, the dumb dog had gone under the deck before and had gotten stuck, so I was mad. Now you see that my nickname was perfect for this dog. My hour of peace was destroyed. I pulled up the lose boards and there right under me was a large possum and about a foot in front of it was the dumb dog. They were screaming at each other sort of, I yelled at the dog to shut up and I moved away so that my shadow was not casting over the deck anymore. I was going to let the possum climb out and go back to wherever it came from. Well the possum seem to understand that this was his chance to leave, so it started to climb out from under the deck, but the dumb dog had other ideas. He decided he wanted to taste the possum before it left, so he reached up and started to bite the possum on the butt and the possum turned to bite the dog on the face. Remember now I was very angry and I had a hammer in my hand and all I saw were these very sharp possum teeth heading right towards the dog's eye. Without thinking about it really I hit that possum with the hammer right between the ears, instantly I had one dead possum laying on the deck. The dumb dog ducked way back under the deck, I swear he truly thought he was next to get smashed on the head with the hammer. I wanted to believe me, I was very angry at him. I knew however that killing the family dog would most likely cost me my job and maybe even my career. I threw the hammer down on the deck, I was very upset, killing the possum was not part of my plans. I paced around for a few minutes in tears trying to decided what in heaven's name to do now. I didn't want the boys to come downstairs and find a dead possum on the deck. Then I heard the answer to my prayers, the sound of the trash truck coming down the street. I ran into the house and got a trash bag and went back outside and picked up the possum by the tail and put it in the trash bag. Then I ran around the house and put it in the trash can on the curb. When I came back around the house to the backyard, the dumb dog was still hiding under the deck. I yelled at him to get his furry butt out of there now. He came out and ran out into the yard as dar away from me as he could possibly get and he stayed there for the rest of the day. The father had to shake a bag of potato chips, the dog's favorite treat, to get him to come back in long after dark. I put the boards back in the deck and put the hammer and screwdriver back in the drawer. I sat down hoping for maybe a few minutes of peace, but then I heard the boys waking up from their nap. I stood up and looked out into the backyard and said dumb dog. The funniest part of this story is after the boys got up. The mother called home from the ladies locker room after her work out. This is again before the average person had a cell phone, but actually the story would still be the same even if she had a cell phone. She called home to check on things from a public pay phone in the locker room. I wish I could have seen the faces of the other women, who couldn't help but over hear her side of the conversation. When I told her about the dog and the possum under the deck, she was saying things like, "you killed it, oh my God!" I can't even begin to imagine what those other women were thinking. In situations like that, even today cell phones, if you are sitting close to someone who is talking, it is impossible not to overhear what they are saying even if you don't want to. That story is still to this one day of that mother's favorites to tell people. How her nanny killed a possum with a hammer.

The first year was great. The boys were very attached to me and I was very attached to them. The older boy who was three and a half years old by this point loved for me to tell him what he called "Texas stories" before bed time. all of these were stories my grandmother once told me. One of his favorites was about the little dog my father had as a boy. My grandparents raised chickens back then and with chickens and chicken feed comes mice and rats. One day my grandmother walked into the bathroom and found a mouse trapped in the bathtub. She quickly ran into the living room yelling "rats, rats!" Their little dog knew exactly what that meant, my grandmother put the now very excited little dog into the bathtub. She then stood back and watched them slip and slide around the tub until the little dog caught and killed the mouse. There were several stories he loved to hear. I asked him not to long ago if he remembered the Texas stories and how much he loved them, He said that he didn't remember and wanted to hear one.

When the boys were three and a half and one years old, the mother got a new job. She would get home from her new job just in time to do bedtime with the boys. For the older boy this was great, one on one snuggle time with mom. The one year old thought and felt very differently about the entire situation. She would come home and we would all go upstairs, I would get the the three year old settled in his bed with all of his stuffed friends and books and all. He had to have a full sized bed so that all of his stuffed friends would have room to sleep with him. He would sit there quietly and play and look at books until his mother came in. Then I would take the one year old and change his diaper and get him ready for bed. In the meantime she would be in her room changing her clothes and then she would come in to sit and rock and read to the one year old. She would sit down in the rocker and I would put him down on her lap. He would scream and cry and reach for me like I was putting down on a complete stranger's lap. I would tell him you're okay, I love you and I will see you in the morning. I would quickly leave the room and close the door. I would maybe get half way down the stairs and then he would appear at the top of the stairs, crying and reaching for me. I would walk back up to him and pick him up. The mother would come with his favorite blanket and teddy bear. The toddler would reach over and take them from her and snuggle into me. She would laugh and smile and kiss him goodnight and say thanks Carol to me and go to the three year old. I will forever have the utmost respect for her. I know I couldn't be that way if it were my child rejecting me like that. I am happy to report that they now have a very close and wonderful relationship. And just let me brag a little, this little one year old boy is now a graduate of West Point.

In those days I would talk to Mom and Dad about once a week. When I did I would tell them all about the kids and what was going on. My father never cared much for the people I worked for. He just couldn't understand how in the world a parent would want to hire a stranger to come in and raise their children. The deal with the one year old only wanting me at bedtime didn't help my father's opinion of my employers that is for sure. Sadly Daddy didn't get to meet this family face to face. I think that would have changed his mind about them. My mother who been to visit me several times in the last several years, she has never met this family face to face, it just never works out. Dad only got to meet one of my families and he really enjoyed that. My only wish is that all of my families could have had the chance to meet him.

The one year old now closer to two year old was starting to talk. He developed an interesting name for me, he called me "Gie." I am not exactly sure where or how he came up with it but he used it loudly on a daily basis. Everyone who knew him and me knew what Gie meant. That was one of the few words that he would say that we understood. One of his favorite ways to use my name he gave me was when he woke up from his nap, he would stand up in his crib and yell "Gie, Gie!" When I would open his bedroom door, he would jump up and down and smile and say holding his little arms out, "Gie" His lack of speech skills got a lot of attention. It was soon discovered that his ear infections, which he had countless ones since he was an infant, had caused poor drainage and he was not hearing well at all. It was decided to put tubes in his ears. The tubes ended his ear infections and with a little help his speech problems ended as well.

It was right before this that back home in Amarillo, my father's health began to go down. I had decided that I could no longer stand to be so far away from home anymore. So in the early spring of 93 after two years with the little boys, I returned to Texas to help care for my Dad. I had hope of finding a nanny position closer to home. I did find one in the Dallas area, but it only lasted the summer. I soon came to the conclusion that there was no such thing as a live-in nanny jobs in Texas. I will never regret that move back to home though, because it gave me time with Dad that I wouldn't have had otherwise, memories that I will cherish forever.

CHAPTER SIX

DEALE

Finally in November of that year, I had to return to the DC area for a good paying nanny position. The DC area was at that time the nanny capital, there were more nannies there than almost anywhere else is the US. This is also where I learned a hard lesson. I learned never ever to agree to a job with only a phone interview. You must meet them face to face, see their house and their lifestyle. You would think that by this point this is a lesson I would have long since learned. I guess everyone can be kind of stupid sometimes. I returned to a family with one small baby girl. They lived far out from the city, close to the bay in Maryland. In fact the bay was in their backyard. It was a beautiful old house. The father was a doctor and the mother was a speech therapist. They were very nice people and the baby girl was adorable, but they had what I would call strange or odd ideas about nannies. They insisted that I wear dress slacks and nice blouses while I working, dress like I was working in an office, not taking care of a baby. I could understand this dress code if they lived in the White House or something, but they lived in the big middle of nowhere. No hardly ever came over during the day, except the maid once a week and she was expected to dress in nice clothes as well to clean their house. I think that most of these ideas came from the mother. I felt as though I was not consider to be part of the family but just an employee or one could even go as far to say just a second class citizen. I just dealt with it for about 3 or 4 months. I guess in hopes that things might get better and because I loved the baby girl.

It all came to a head one night when the parents and I had a big fight about the situation. I said how could they possibly expect me to be

happy and feel at home when the only room in the house I was allowed
to really be myself was in my room. I remember being very upset and in
tears. They said they wanted me to be happy and feel at home, that this
was my home. They said that they never met to hurt me. The situation
kind of worked itself out for a while, but I wanted out and I was looking
for that way out when one day my prayers were answered. The mother
came to me and said that they had decided that they didn't want a
live-in nanny anymore. That was the best news my ears had ever heard,
I felt like jumping up and down and screaming for joy, but I didn't, not
in front of the mother. She said that I could stay and work for them
through the summer until I found another job. She thought it would
take me all summer to find a new job, boy, did she ever misjudge that
one. I contacted the nanny agency and began to talk to and interview
with other families. One day I talked to this lady who had two or three
small kids. We hit it off instantly, we talked and laughed for almost two
hours on the phone. I was so happy and excited after we hung up the
phone. A chance to be a part of a happy loving family, well you know
what they say about first impressions. The nanny profession has taught
me one thing and that is never trust first impressions. A few days later
I had an interview with this wonderful family. I found out why this
would not be that perfect family I was searching for. Understand they
were very nice people and adorable kids, but for reasons that I am not
sure of, they had been through six nannies in a little over a year. That is
one of those things that should set off all kinds of alarms in a nanny's
head, it sure did in mine. I was nice and supportive to this family, I
do remember thinking about those adorable little kids and wishing I
could help them. The next phone call I got was from a lady who was
a doctor. She must have called me from her office, because she was in
full doctor mode. You know what I mean, that don't talk just listen
because I am God routine. Almost any doctor who has been one for
more then a year or so usually develops that attitude, I realize that there
are a few exceptions. We talked for a few minutes, she told me she had
two little boys and a nanny who had been there for almost three years.
The nanny was leaving to go back to school and finish what she started
nearly three years before. We scheduled an interview and the phone call
ended. I remember very clearly thinking as I hung up the phone, man,
I really don't want to work for that lady. She sounded cold and tough,
almost mean on the phone. It was almost like she was angry that she

had to waste her time trying to find another nanny for her children, which it was my impression were just in the way of her career. My first impression of her and her family life could not have been more wrong. Like I said never trust first impressions of people, they are always wrong. The lady I met at that interview was nothing like that, she was sweet, outgoing and fun and a wonderful mother. The entire family was like that, I fell head over heels in love with the little boys from the start. The youngest one had blonde curly hair and these amazing blue eyes and the best belly laugh. The older boy was adorable and very smart and he had the best imagination. At that interview, I knew that I had found that perfect family. The interview went very well, I left thinking I had it made. They called me back a day or so later for a second interview that was better than the first. I was offered the job, which of course I said yes instantly. I went back to the family by the bay with the one baby girl and told them that I had another job and that I was moving out on the upcoming weekend. This was only 4 or 5 days after she told me that they no longer wanted a live-in nanny. The mother looked at me and said in kind of a panic stricken voice, I thought you would be here to work for us at least through the summer. I said no, you said that I could stay here through the summer if I needed to, but I don't need to and I am moving out this weekend. She started to say something and I just looked at her and said you broke the contract, we are done and I walked away. I remember being very happy and excited, I was packing my stuff that night until well after midnight. I moved out that weekend with the help of a dear friend. I remember that Saturday morning, the mother offered me and my friend breakfast, we both said no thanks, we need to hit the road. I walked over to the baby in her walker and I picked her up. She was about 7 months old at the time. I held her tight and kissed her little cheek several times and whispered in her little ear that I would love her with all of my heart always. I knew that I would likely never see her again. Which turned out to be true, she is one of the few that I don't have contact with today. I handed her to her moth and we walked out of the door. That was hard and it hurt to have to walk away. Knowing that I wouldn't most likely see her again made walking away that much harder. A nanny must go into a job knowing that she will someday have to let go and maybe before she is ready.

CHAPTER SEVEN

THE PERFECT FAMILY

While all of this was going one, my parents back in Texas were making plans of their own. All of this was taking place in May of 1994. My parents were to celebrate their 40th wedding anniversary that December. They had decided that they wanted all four of us to be home with them for one week sometime during that year. They wanted to have the whole family together for a week to be their anniversary present. My brothers and sister and I got the funniest letter from our parents about their plans. Mom and Dad were not trying to be silly, they were serious. I was extremely worried if I could even be there or not, I mean most people don't ask to take a week's vacation right after they start a new job. I told Mom on the phone that their timing couldn't be worse for me and that this might not work out like they planned. I think my Dad said something like show them the letter and tell them that it is required and they can take care of their own children for a week. Remember I told you that my Dad had little respect for the families that I worked for. So I did what he said and showed my new employers the letter from my parents, but I didn't tell them that it was required or that they could take care of their own children, I didn't think they would think that was funny.

That is when I found out just how wonderful things were going to be with this family. They were wonderful and understanding and thought my parent's plan was great. I remember the mother laughed and got tears in her eyes when she read the letter. I think she thought how wonderful and lucky I was to be part of such a close family. I knew she wished and hoped that her family could be that way someday too.

So I took off to Amarillo for my parent's celebration week. I remember feeling high like I was on top of the world when I flew home. I knew that I found the perfect family and life was great. All four of us were there as requested or should I say ordered. The oldest my sister and her husband and sons, my younger brother and his girlfriend and my older brother were all there. We all still talk about that week and what fun we had just being together. I can't remember seeing my parents so happy, especially Dad, he always wanted all of us home. That was the last time we were all together, Dad passed away just two years later. That event would again prove to me and my Mom just how wonderful this family is.

When I returned the job began. The hours were long, longer than most other nanny positions. The only exception would be the single mother in New York. Both of these parents are career people. He is an engineer and she is a doctor. They usually didn't walk in the door until seven or later at night. When I started the first nanny had the boys on a schedule where the boys would go down for nap around two and sleep until five or six o'clock at night. She had good reason for doing things this way, the parents would have time to spend with the boys at night. The boys would be up until all hours of the night, most nights until at least ten. In the old fashion home I grew up in, bed time was by eight or nine at the latest. We were always in bed at a reasonable hour, so my parents had time together. This deal with the kids up and running around until all hours of the night was something I couldn't deal with at all. So I laid down the law, I told the parents that the kids would nap from two to four o'clock every day and no later. I hoped that my willingness to boss people around wouldn't cost me my job. I am a total control freak, I admit. I knew that the older boy would be starting school soon and the schedule they had was not conducive to that. The parents understood this as well, thank goodness. So if the parents wanted to spend time with the kids in the evening, they had to come home earlier that's all, because bedtime was at eight o'clock sharp. My plans or should I say my demands went over better than I thought and I didn't lose my job. Actually I think I earned some respect for making this job mine and not the former nanny's anymore. I had big shoes to fill in the boy's eyes, especially the older boy. He was at first not happy about the only nanny he had ever known leaving him and he wasn't sure he liked me at all. I really had my job cut out for me to earn his trust and love. I told him that it was okay if he was sad and if he missed her, that I understood that. He slowly learned that I was fun and he could trust me and we grew closer with every passing day.

The mother and I also worked out a deal where she would make up weekly menus and I would at least get the dinner started for the parents. If she cam home early enough she would help me finish making the dinner. I always fed the boys before they came home from work. Most of the time I had the boys fed and their dinner made before either one of them walked in the door. On most nights, the boys would be about done with their dinner, I would hear the garage door start to open. I would say to the boys, Dad's home, go downstairs, see Daddy. They would leap up from their chairs at the table and run around the corner and downstairs, yelling Daddy, Daddy all the way. The father would come in the door, he would put his briefcase and coat down and the games would begin. I will always love and respect him for that.

Near the end of that first summer, the boys were exposed to chicken poxes from the little summer day camp the older boy was going to. Without fail within a couple of weeks, the older boy had the chicken pox. This happened about three weeks before the entire family including me were supposed to go on vacation. That is the way it always happens, isn't it. The kids get sick right before vacation. That just proves what I have always said and that is that the Good Lord has a very funny sense of humor. I knew that the younger boy would get the chicken poxes after being exposed to it twenty four seven for about two weeks. It was funny, one night the father came home and sat down with the older boy and began counting his spots. They counted every single chicken pox I think, the older boy really got a kick of it. If memory serves me correctly they counted about one hundred twenty seven chicken pox. I was with this family again not long ago and of course the boys are now grown up and in college. I asked the father and the older boy if they remembered counting the chicken poxes, they didn't. The father said that that sounded like something he would probably do though. I knew that the little guy would get the chicken pox before we went on vacation. The parents were hoping that he would not come down with it until after we got there. The mother's parents had a cabin in the northern woods of Wisconsin. The boys called it Grandpa's park. Sadly I never got to go up there with them. So the parents and I started checking the little guy's tummy every morning for spots. He thought it was a great game of course. He would come downstairs and mommy and Carol would ask him to show off his tummy, what could be better when you are about twenty three months old.

We were supposed to fly up to Madison and then drive to the cabin. I was really looking forward to it honestly, but I knew that it wasn't going to happen. I never packed a thing in the suitcase. I knew that we couldn't expose everyone in the airport and on the plane to chicken poxes. That is just not right, plus it is dangerous. So the debate continued about what to do if and hoping and praying that he didn't get it. A couple of days prior to departure, I sat down with the parents and I told them that I would stay home with the little guy if he got the chicken pox so that they could take the older boy and go on their vacation. They were grateful and said that they would consider that option if necessary.

The morning before we were to leave, the parents were so excited that there were still no signs of chicken poxes. The older boy was over his chicken poxes and they thought their prayers were answered. Understand I still have not packed a thing because I knew very well that the younger boy had the chicken pox. I knew he and I were not going to Grandpa's park. So on that faithful morning, the little guy came bouncing down the stairs in his pajamas and like so many mornings before the mother and I asked to see his tummy. He grinned with delight and pulled up his shirt and there were chicken pox just like I knew all along there would be. The mother and I looked at each other and I could not stop myself and I said I told you so. The father came downstairs and we had a meeting and talked about what the options were. I reminded them of what I said I would do. The parents told me that I didn't have to and I told them that it was okay, I could take care of things. They were grateful and then set out to make sure I had everything that we might need. The mother made up a list of friends that would help if needed as well. Believe it or not I wasn't to worried about it, I was pretty sure I could deal with things on my own. For what its worth, I did manage to handle things all on my own. There is not much that makes a person feel better then when you can handle a tough situation all on your own.

So the parents and the older boy went off on vacation and I began to watch the chicken pox spread all over the baby. He was covered from the top of hie little head down to his little toes. He had the worst case of chicken pox I had ever seen. He was running a fever, sometimes as much as 102 degrees. The first two nights we didn't sleep much, he was totally miserable. He wasn't eating much either, the only intake was his bottles of milk. We were before he got sick trying to get him off the bottle, but I had pretty much given that up for now. I was letting him have as many as he wanted. The bottle was also how I was sneaking his medicine into him without a fuss. Then there was the oatmeal baths, I'll bet he took at least twenty of them and half of those were in the middle of the night. He would wake up crying and miserable and a warm oatmeal bath was the only thing I found that would calm him back down. Sometimes he would be awake for quite a while before he would fall back to sleep. Finally on the third day things began to get better. We slept all night and he started eating more solid foods and best of all his fever went away.

Bless his little heart all of this was taking place the week of his second birthday. I think it was the third or fourth day that was actually his birthday. On his birthday he was no longer contagious and I made a special point to take him to the toy store and get some sort of present for him. He picked out a neat little truck which he didn't let go of for several days. I talked to the parents several times during that week. They said many times that they would come home if I wanted them to, I told them it was okay and we were fine., but it was nice knowing that they would if I wanted. He completely recovered from the chicken poxes and the rest of the family returned home from their trip. That fall the older boy started preschool. It was walking distance from the house. So everyday twice a day I would pack the toddler in the stroller and walk up to the preschool. The mother wanted the toddler to go to some kind of school as well and this school didn't have space for him. So she found another preschool for the boys to attend. Let explain one thing, the mother of this family is a doctor and the father is an engineer. When they research something it has been researched thoroughly. I have seen this father take a month or more to research car models, before he picks one he knows everything possible to know about every car. To make a long story shorter, they researched paid off, they found a great preschool. This school was a little farther away, my days of packing the stroller and walking to school were over for now.

That summer both boys went to summer camp at the new school. The toddler, now a two year old, loved it. When I took the boys to camp, they had the parents drop the kids off at the gate to the playground. They put name tags on the kids. Understand one thing none of these kids going to this summer camp was more than five years old, these are little kids. Instead of using stickers or masking tape stuck on the kid's back. They started out using safety pins and pinning the name tags on, which we didn't have a problem with at all. Believe it or not some goofy parent did have a problem with it, they actually complained about the tiny holes the pins were making in their kid's shirt. Give me a break, what do you send your little preschooler off to summer camp in? Bloomingdale's finest right? So the preschool changed the tags, remember now we were dropping off the kids at the gate to the playground. The school decided to use name tags on strings around the kid's necks. Excuse me but I am the only one who sees the danger in that. I dearly hope not, I couldn't believe that this preschool would actually do that. I told the teacher to use the old pinned on ones on my boys and then I called the mother. She couldn't believe it either, I was happy that she saw the danger too. In my years as a nanny I have found that sometimes you and the parents don't see eye to eye on things that could be dangerous to the kids. The mother quickly put a stop to the name tags on strings, I think she found other parents who were upset as well.

On funny thing happened that first summer the boys went to summer camp at that preschool. One morning I was getting the boys ready for camp. The older boys is very much like his father, he likes everything to be just right. The younger boy is let's just say he is a free spirit. That morning the younger boy has his heart set on wearing this one shirt to camp. It was a football jersey from one of the NFL teams, but he didn't have a pair of shorts that went with it well. So I found an old pair of jeans that had a hole in the knee of them. I asked the mother if I could turn them into cutoffs for the little guy to wear to camp. She didn't mind that at all and thought he would look cute. So I turned them into cutoffs and he happily put them on with his jersey and went downstairs to breakfast. The younger boy was sitting at the table in the kitchen eating his breakfast when the older boy came down. His shirt and shorts matched perfectly and his shirt was tucked in just right and his little socks were folded neatly around his ankles. He looked perfect, just the way he wanted to. He walked into the kitchen, stopped in the middle and looked at his little brother and said with his hands on his hips, "are you really going to let him wear that to camp?" I had to bite my bottom lip so I wouldn't laugh at him and I told him that his little brother looked just fine to go to camp. The older boy rolled his eyes and shook his head and sat down at the table for breakfast. This little boy was about 4 four years old then. How many four year old little boys do you know that give a darn what their little brothers are wearing to summer camp, most would not even notice, well this kid did. Little kids are so funny sometimes with the things they say and do. Parents and teachers and care givers often have holes in their lower lips from all the biting that they do to avoid laughing out loud.

Later that summer there was a big thunder storm one late afternoon. It rained really hard and the wind blew and it hailed some to I think. The storm also made the power go out as well. The boys loved this because it made for a great game of hide-n-go seek in the house. When the storm was over and the lights came back on, I walked out on the deck to smell the clean fresh air after the storm. As I walked out on the deck I could hear some birds making a big fuss about something. I got to the railing and looked over down to the patio below. I could see a bird flying low around one of the patio chairs and I could see a small baby bird flopping around under the chair. The poor mama bird was trying with everything she had to save her baby. I went back inside and told the boys to come outside with me. I got a plastic container and we went outside to the patio. The mom bird flew away up into a nearby tree still crying for her baby, bless her heart. I scooped up the baby bird in the plastic container. The boys were fascinated with the little bird and asking me all sorts of questions, the biggest of which was what are you going to with it now. I began to look around to see if I could see a nest nearby. While we were searching the father came home, I explained to him what had happened and what I was doing. He quickly put his stuff in the house and joined in the search for the nest. Right up by the deck was a huge evergreen tree, the father was sure that the nest was in that tree. He got the ladder from the garage and climbed up to have a look. Sure enough he was right, there was a nest, he reached his hand in to pull the branch over closer to him and then he realized that there was also a large black snake in the tree. He yelled something, I don't really recall what and came quickly down off the ladder. I do know that whatever he yelled, it wasn't a four letter word. This father would never ever consider saying anything like that in front of his little boys. Right then it began to rain again a little and we all went back inside to wait it out and decide what to do with this baby bird. The baby bird's brother or sister had become the snake's dinner. I knew two things for sure as I sat there in the kitchen holding the baby bird, first the momma bird would not return to a nest where a snake had been and second I knew that could locate someone who has the skilled and could raise the baby bird and eventually set it free. It stopped raining again, there was a beautiful rainbow that appeared just over the trees as the sun began to set. I decided to get that snake out of that tree. I can't explain why I had decided to get the snake out, but I just knew it was something I had to do. The mother came home while we were waiting for the rain to stop. The boys just had to tell her in gross detail the entire story about the poor baby bird and the big black snake in the tree. She announced in no uncertain term that she wanted nothing to do with it and she disappeared up to her room and closed the door. I put the container with the baby bird on the kitchen table and announced that I was going to get that snake out of that tree. The father looked at me in total shock and amazement and said you are" The father and the boys followed me back outside. The older boy saying "Oh cool, how are you going to get him, Carol?" The father made it very clear to me that he was very worried about the snake bitting me. I knew and I told him that a snake can't stop and drop something once it starts eating. I think I learned that from Animal Planet and that Crocodile guy. The father said okay but he would rather that I just left it alone. I climbed up the ladder and looked in and there was a large black snake. They are pretty common in the Maryland and Virginia suburbs, they can and will bite, but they are harmless. I like snake unlike most women, namely the mother of this family and through the years I have learned a lot about them. Snakes look at the world very simply, if it is bigger than me I am afraid of it and if it is smaller than me I am going to eat it. So needless to say I knew I was not on the snake's food list. The snake was wrapped about half way around the tree, he was laid out on several branches and as I thought had a mouthful of baby bird. I reached in and took hold of the snake's middle and pulled him out of the tree. The father and the boys were standing several feet back from the ladder as I climbed down with the snake wiggling wildly in one hand. This snake was not at all happy about my decision to remove him from the tree during the middle of his dinner. The father asked me what my plans were for the snake now. I said that I was going to put it in the ten gallon aquarium we had in the garage. We had hermit crabs at one point, they had all since died. The aquarium had a metal mess top and I knew it was a safe place to put the snake while he finished his dinner. Also I wanted the boys to get a closer look at the snake, this was a learning experience for sure. We went into the garage and I put the snake in the aquarium and put the mess top on it with a couple of bricks on top so the snake couldn't push the top off. I told the boys that we needed to leave the snake alone for a little while and let him finish his dinner. I said that we shouldn't handle him much while he was eating. we went back inside for a while to check on the baby bird. The boys ran upstairs to tell their mother all about the snake and how Carol pulled him out of the tree. She didn't want to see or hear or especially touch this invader into her snake free world. After an hour or so we went back to check on the snake. We walked into the garage and there was an active large black snake looking for a way out of the prison we had put him in. He had a large lump in his middle where the baby bird was now. I admit that I was a little nervous about trying to get this now angry snake out of the aquarium without getting bit. I took a deep breathe, planned my attack and I careful and slowly raised the lid. I used the to kind of block the snake in one corner of the tank. Then I quickly reached in and grabbed him around the neck right below his head. The snake wrapped his body around my arm to try to get away. The father and the boys were watching closely, that is another reason why I was nervous about getting him out without getting bit. I had something to prove the father, that I did actually know what in the world I was doing and that I could do it. I must admit that it felt real good to be able to do it on the first try with them watching. Moments like that are always good for one's ego, you know. As I lifted him out I adjusted my grip around his neck and got my other hand around his body so I could control him better. The father asked me how I planned to kill the snake. He said that he had a brick that would work if I wanted to do it that way. I looked at him kind of in shock that he would even suggest such a thing in front of the boys. I told him that I had no intention of killing the snake. I said that the snake was harmless and the main reason that there weren't any mice around his house and I said you don't get the death sentence for eating your dinner. I told him that if he wanted to kill the snake he could do it himself and I held out the snake for him to take from me. I said that I wouldn't have anything to do with killing it. He looked at me and said no and stepped back. He asked what I was going to do with it then. I said that I was going to set it free in the woods behind the house. I said to the boys come on lets go set him free so he can be on his way. I felt bad about talking to the father that way, but I felt strongly that killing the snake with the boys watching was not the right thing to do and not the lesson I wanted them to learn from this experience. I wanted the boys to learn to love and respect wild life, not to kill it and I think that is what the father really wanted as well. Understand if this snake was dangerous to the boys or anyone around, I would have wanted to get rid of it. I would have made sure the boys understood why and it wouldn't have happened in front of them. So we set out to the woods behind the house, I was carrying the snake. I stopped in the backyard to show the boys the snake. I showed them just how really beautiful this creature was. The snake had a shiny silver under side, it almost looked like it had been polished. His eyes had this very delicate pattern in gold around the edge of his eye ball, like someone had taken a tiny paint brush and painted his eyes. Snakes get a bad rap from humans, it all started in the Bible. Women especially see snakes as something that is slimly and gross and scary and just out to bite you. You couldn't be more wrong, snakes are very beautiful fascinating creatures. Snakes would really rather not have anything to do with the human race and who can blame them. I wanted the boys to learn not to be afraid of it. They wanted to touch the snake, I said yes but don't touch the lump in the middle. We talked about the snake, his tongue going in and out of his mouth, his eyes and his shiny under side. The father quickly understood what a wonderful learning experience I was creating for the boys with this snake. He touched it and joined in the conversation about it. We walked a little further into the woods and I said this looks like a good spot right here by this bush. I let the boys touch him one time and say goodbye and I put him on the ground. We watched as he quickly slithered away out of sight. As we walked back to the house, the boys were talking about their snake adventure with the snake. I felt a sense of pride swell up inside of me, because I knew I had an impact on the boys. I done something that they won't soon forget. Actually I think the father learned something about snakes that day too. To make this story even better, I will tell you two things, first I did find some experienced person to take care of and raise the baby bird and second several years later the family cut down that evergreen tree and used it for a Christmas tree, nest and all. They invited me over to see the tree in their living room all decorated. It was really cool, we took pictures and talked about that amazing day.

That fall both of the boys were in preschool, it was a great preschool and both of the boys felt happy and safe there. The older boy was now four years and the younger boy was now three years old. They were in this big class room together but in separate groups. Everything was rocking right along until that winter when we had a big snow storm and as expected the school parking lot was plowed so that parents and teachers could park. The snow plows made these huge mounds of snow that they pushed near the edge of the lot by the chain link fence. So the next day the kids were in school, the playground was still covered with snow. The teachers wanted the kids to be able to play outside, so when it was above freezing, they took the kids out on the parking lot to play with balls, bikes and such. Which is fine, I understand the need to get little kids outside to run off steam, but they also allowed the kids to climb on these huge piles of snow. I will never forget how that made me feel the first time I saw them doing that. I felt instantly angry and extremely afraid all at the same time, because those kids had two ways to seriously hurt themselves. The first was to fall off this huge pile of snow down on on top of a chain link fence and the second was to fall down to the blacktop parking lot. Understand these piles of snow were at least seven feet tall, maybe as much as eight feet and the chain link fence below was four feet high I think. I quickly went and got my boys off the piles of snow and instructed them and their teacher that they were not allowed up there again for any reason. I left the boys riding bikes on the parking lot for a few minutes and walked into the office to talk to the director or principal. I was very mad and in shock that this licensed preschool was actually allowing this to take place. There isn't much else that upsets or makes me furious instantly then when I see someone stupid adult carelessly putting a child's life at stake. Like when you see people taking little kids across a very busy street in the middle, because they think their child is safe because he or she is in their arms or they are just too lazy to walk to the corner and the light. If you want to risk your own life, fine be my guest, but you have no right to risk the life of a child even if that child is yours. You may have given birth to that child, but the child's life belongs to him not to you. That is how I felt when I saw the kids playing on the huge piles of snow. I was glad I could put a stop to my boys playing up there. Anyway before I walked into the office, I stopped and took a deep breathe and tried to plan out in my head what I was going to say and how I was going to say it to the director. I went in and asked if she had a moment to talk, she said yes and we sat down. First I asked if she even knew that they were allowing the kids to playing on the piles of snow. She said she did and said little kids love snow and it is impossible to keep them out of it. I explained why I believed that allowing the kids to play on the huge piles of snow was so dangerous. I told her that I could easily in vision one of those kids either falling down to the black top parking lot and hitting their head or falling backwards off and impaling themselves on the chain link fence. What completely blew my mind and made me even more angry and afraid was the fact that she didn't see those dangers and didn't seem to care at all. She told me that she would be in touch with the boy's mother. She knew that I was just the nanny and my opinion of the situation didn't matter or at least that is what she thought. I left before I got really angry and out of control, because even though I knew it would make me feel really good to really chew her out, I also knew that she wasn't worth losing my job over and that mother would be on my side. I was really upset when I walked out of her office, but I knew that I had to pull myself together for the boys. I got the boys and told them that we were going to see mommy at her office. I felt that she needed to know what was happening and how upset I was. Plus I wanted her to hear my side of the story first. I wasn't sure exactly what director might tell here. Covering your own butt, you know. Here again this family would prove to me just how wonderful they are. The mother was of course surprised to see us. As tears began to roll down my cheeks, I told her what I saw at the preschool and how afraid I was that a child might get seriously hurt. I also told her how the director just carelessly dismissed my concerns like they didn't matter because she knew that I was just the nanny and not the mother. She told me I was right and that she would back me up no matter what and that my concerns did matter to her and she hugged me. She also told me that she was sorry that I was so upset by it all. The next morning the director of the preschool called the mother to complain about me and to tell the mother to please control her nanny. Well the mother set her straight, she told her that whatever I said was what she felt as well and that she should listen to me and show me the respect that I deserved. That afternoon the mother came home early and told me what she had said to the director of the preschool. I don't remember if all the kids were made to stay off the piles of snow or not, but I do remember the director and the teachers started listening to me and taking what I said to heart.

It wasn't long after that we learned that her college was doing very well in football and had hight hopes of going to a bowl game in January. One Saturday Northwestern her college was winning a big game on television and the mother announced to the entire family that if Northwestern goes to the Rose Bowl game, we were all going to the Rose bowl game too. Amazingly Northwestern continued their winning ways and they did win a trip to the Rose Bowl. So plans were made for all of us to go in January. Actually what ended up happening was that we left for California the morning after I returned from Texas after Christmas. I got in real late that night and we were leaving very early the next morning. I remember being totally exhausted and wishing with all that I had that I didn't have to go on this trip. Anyway, we all loaded up in the mini van before the sun was even close to being up and went back to the airport where I had been just a few hours before. Luck was on my side that morning, because the parents wanted to sit with the boys. So I got to sit by myself and sleep. When we arrived at the airport in Los Angeles, I was rested and ready to deal with it I thought. I had never been to the L.A. airport before, wow, what an insanely crazy place. My biggest fear has always been losing a child somewhere and the L.A. airport was the prime place to do that. I have never lost a child and I wasn't going to start at the airport in the company of the parents. We walked for what seemed like hours to baggage claim and then some more walking to find our bags. Which to my amazement we found them rather easily, then we went to the rent car place to rent a car. All of this time I am working my butt off not to lose one of the kids and also to keep them happy and somewhat entertained as well. When we finally got the rental car, we drove to the mother's aunt's house in San Diego. Somehow I am not exactly sure how, we managed to get through the airport and all and to San Diego and the aunt's house without getting hopelessly lost or losing a child. The mother's aunt was an interesting lady, very outgoing and full of energy and fun, I liked her right away. After we got to her house we all pretty much crashed for the night. The next morning we went to the San Diego zoo, the amazing San Diego zoo. It is totally incredible you really need an entire week to see the whole zoo. I am very sad to report to you now that I don't remember all of the animals we saw that day, but I know that we didn't come close to seeing it all. I'll bet you have a pretty good guess as to the animals we did see, lions, tiger and bears and elephants and such. It is a beautiful place and very well kept, clean and I bet more amazing today. We all had a blast I think that was my favorite part of the whole trip. The next day we went to Disney Land, oh my goodness were the boys excited. It was great watching their eyes light up as we walked through there. I talked the father into riding this ride with me. It wasn't a roller coaster exactly but it spun around and I am pretty sure it went upside down as well. I love it when he turned a shade of green and he didn't enjoy it at all. The evil side of me really enjoyed watching him turned green. The only part that wasn't much fun for me anyway was the small world ride, you know the one I mean. You right this train like thing through this castle like building. Inside there are all these Disney characters from movies, mostly Snow White characters I think. The entire time you are riding through looking at all of this cute stuff, they are playing loudly I might add "it's a small world after all" over and over again. For most adults even me who truly loves kids music, this song gets real old after the very first verse. The next say we went to Pasadena where the Rose Bowl is and the parade. The mother's aunt came with us and we all stayed in a hotel together. The parents and the boys in one room and me and the aunt in another room, which was fine by me, the aunt and I hit it off from the start. The next morning was the parade and the game. The aunt decided that she wanted to hang out with the boys and take them to some other amusement park instead of going to the game, I loved because that meant that I got to go to the game. We were in bed early that night I told the boys as we tucked them in bed that tomorrow was going to be another exciting day. I fell asleep pretty quickly and was awaken very early in the morning by a sound. I laid there for a moment trying to figure out what in the world I was hearing and what time it was as well. The room was still very dark so I knew it was before sunrise. I realized the sound I was hearing was the wind blowing very hard. The aunt asked me if I was awake and I said yes, then she says that the Santa Anna winds are blowing very hard and the power is out in the hotel and from what she could see out of the window all over town as well. I hate the sound of wind blowing. I always have I guess it is because I grew up in the heart of tondo country. We all got up and got dressed, it was about four in the morning. The hotel was completely dark as we started to make our way very slowly to the staircase. In the hall we found a hotel security guard, the aunt confiscated his flashlight. It was really very funny the way she man-handled him. She told him that we needed it to get our little boys down the stairs and that was that. That poor guy never had a chance and didn't put up much an argument. We made our way slowly down several flights of stairs. The boys thought it was cool to be walking around in this big hotel in the dark. By the time we got down and out of the hotel it was close to six in the morning. We walked to an open bagel and breakfast sandwich place and got food. We ate our breakfast as we continued to walk to our seats in the grand stand to watch the parade with tons and tons of other people. I don't remember ever seeing so many people in one place in my entire life. The mother had ordered the entire family Northwestern purple sweatshirts to wear to the parade and to the game, so we were pretty hard to miss. We sat down and the boys and I began to talk about all the different people we saw and the many different languages we began to hear. People watching has always been one of my favorite past times. It is always amazing to me what people will choose to wear in public. I am not sure which it is either they just don't care or they really think they look good. The boys and I had a great time laughing and making fun quietly of some of the people we saw while waiting for the parade. We didn't have to wait very long, the parade started. There is not a television around not even the best HD that can do this parade justice, beautiful, amazing and wonderful are the only words I can think of and spell correctly that can describe this parade. The best part of the parade without question was watching through the eyes and faces of the boys. We talked about everything that went by and of course the father and the older boy talked about how things were made and how they worked as well. The father is an engineer and the older boy is going to be just like his father. When the parade ended, we started walking back towards the hotel with what seemed like all the people in the entire state of California. When we got back to the hotel we had lunch and the boys took a nap. It was easy to get them to take a nap that day, we had been up for hours by noon and there had been a lot of excitement as well. Honestly I think we all ended up taking a nap. After nap time the aunt announced that she really did want to take the boys and play instead of going to the game. They only had three tickets, so her decision was great news to me.

So after nap time the aunt took the happy and excited boys to this other amusement park and the parents and I started walking again to the stadium for the game. Our seats were up in one corner by one of the end zones. I don't think there is a bad seat really in that stadium actually. I was in awe, I was sitting in a stadium that I had seen on television all of my life and knowing that I was at a game that the entire country was watching on television. It was mind blogging to say the least. Like all college games you go to see, we had to stand up the whole game. You could sit down if you wanted to but you just couldn't see anything if you did. The other issue I had was the parents are really not sports fans, they don't watch football normally on television. So they really didn't know much about it. I spent most of the game explaining to the parents what was what and what was happening. To give you a clue as to how much they didn't know about the game of football, the father asked me as the game was just getting started what the guys in the stripes shirts were for? He was asking about the referees. I had to bite my tongue almost in half to keep from laughing real hard in his face and explained to him what their job was. After that every time there was a flag I had to explain what it meant and what was going to happen. The half time show was great too. both school's marching bands were amazing. I never played an instrument in school, but I know that if I did I would have messed up everything on the field because I would have gotten totally lost while marching. How they know where to go, who they are supposed to follow and when is way beyond me. Also when I see a marching band I can't help but think of my mother. She told me that when she was in the marching band in high school, she couldn't march and play at the same time. She said she would just move her fingers like she was playing. I remember standing there looking around and thinking about all my friends and family watching on television and looking for me in the stands. It was one of those once in a life time moments you know. Nannies should feel very blessed when they get opportunities like that. The parents paid for everything on that trip. I must tell you that it is pretty nice when you have a nanny job with a family that wants to and works hard to include you in the family events. This was only the beginning of what this family would do for me. The real test came a few months later. Well the game ended and not the way we wanted it to, Northwestern lost to USC, but they played well and it was good game. The parents and I and what seemed like the rest of the state of California started walking. We were holding on to each other to keep from getting separated, I had a hold of the father's belt loop. It felt like we were a small part of a giant moving thing, like a giant moving snake or something, crazy.

The next morning we headed home. Life was going to return to what we hoped was a normal routine. Normal didn't last long at all. We got home and found that the clothes dryer had decided to die. Then just to make things real interesting the next morning it began to snow and I mean snow!! You can look it up, it was called the blizzard of 96. So I am stuck in the house and there is a ton of dirty laundry to do and no dryer, lovely. Well necessity being the mother of invention, I strung a rope from one end of the basement to the other end and that was my clothes line. After all the laundry was done and the dryer was replaced, it became a great tent for the boys. It was so big that it had two rooms, one of which was big enough for me to stretch out in. The boys and I had a blast in it and I think the boys and I might have camped out in it at least once. Well the snow melted away and spring came which meant we could finally be outside. One of the boy's favorite things to do when the weather was nice was to walk through the woods behind their house. I think it was almost a half a mile down the hill through the woods there was a stream. Most of the stream was only ankle deep and the current wasn't strong at all. It was a great place to be a little boys. They could wade around through the water looking for frogs and little fish and whatever else they could find. We were always on the hunt for dinosaur fossils. The older boy really wanted to find his very own dinosaur fossil. I don't remember for sure if we ever did, but he always looking for one. When we went down there, I could count on spending at least an hour or so and I could count on very dirty little boys as well. I don't mind that part, that is what little boys are supposed to do, right, get real dirty. Our springs and summers were spent playing in the stream and going to the pool. The boys went to summer camp again and I think the family made a trip to Grandpa's park, this time the younger boy got to go.

CHAPTER EIGHT

DAD'S DEATH

That summer I went home to Amarillo to see my family. Dad's health was getting much worse and it was hard seeing him like that. There is muscular dystrophy in my family, my Dad and my older brother had and have myotonic muscular dystrophy. Without going into too much detail, I will tell you that it is one of the diseases Jerry Lewis raises money for every September. I know Jerry Lewis doesn't do it anymore but as far as my family and I are concerned it will always be Jerry Lewis' telethon and Jerry's kids. The disease strikes people late in life and it is getting worse with each generation, that is very obvious in my family. While I was home that summer I tried to spend as much time as possible with Dad. I remember he and I were home alone and we were talking. He was worried about my Mom trying to take care of his mother after he was gone. He didn't want her to do that and told me not to let her and I said to him, Dad how in the world am I supposed to stop her. He laughed and agreed with me. After that vacation ended as I was getting on the plane to fly back I remember worrying if I would ever see Dad alive again and if I would get a chance to say goodbye. That was one of my biggest fears, not getting to say goodbye to him and Mom being home alone and finding him dead or something. With this disease sudden death was a big possibility. Getting back on the plane to return to Washington was the hardest thing I did. I was so scared that he would die before I could get back. The rest of that summer went by pretty much without many problems. Then things went bad in late September. This was when the perfect family I had found proved to me just how wonderful they really are.

In late September my Dad got a bad cold and ended up in the hospital. The dystrophy had damaged his diaphragm and he couldn't exhale the way he should. Therefor the co2 levels would build up in his blood. Mom called me and told me that they were putting him into the hospital. I asked her then if I should come home. She said it is okay for now, if they put him on a ventilator, I will need you here. I told the parents what was happening at home with Mom and Dad. They were understanding and concerned and said that I could go home anytime I needed to. Then one morning a couple of days later Mom calls me, she said that he was now on a ventilator. I remember crying like crazy after talking to Mom. The boys were in school so they were not witness to my sadness. I called the mother at her office after I collected myself and told her what had happened. She said how sorry she was and asked if I was okay and said that she would come home as fast as she could. Both parents came home as soon as they could and they helped me make flight arrangements. We talked about what they could do to help and that I shouldn't worry about anything and just take care of my family. We called Mom and they talked to her. Mom still talks about how touched she was. That afternoon I told the boys about my sick father and that I was going to have to be gone for a while. I didn't go into gross detail with them of course, but I told them that I would be gone for what seemed like forever to them but I would be back and that I loved them very much.

The next day I got on the plane for home, the entire flight I wondered if I would get there in time. Because Amarillo is such a small town, there isn't a direct flight to it. As we were landing in Dallas, I remembered my father's words and had to laugh, he said "you can't go to heaven without going through Dallas first". My Mom had said that one of her friends, Nancy would be there to meet me. After I got my bags and walked passed the security area, I saw Nancy waiting for me. We hugged and she filled me in on what was happening. We went to the hospital and met up with Mom and my grandmother. Honestly the first few days I was there are now all a blur. It has been close to 18 years ago and one's memory does a tendency to fade a little over time. I remember that we spent most of everyday at the hospital, waiting in the waiting room, going in and seeing Dad every two hours for a few minutes. He was in intensive care, so visiting times were limited. I do remember one happy event that happened during that time. One of my best friends had her first baby. I remember thinking just how happy my Dad would be about her first kid. I was was thinking to myself and laughing a little about how he would tease her constantly about it as well. I thought to myself also how Dad and this baby boy were like two ships passing in the night. This beautiful little baby boy just entering the world and my Dad getting ready to pass on to the next life. It was hard to be happy, but on the other hand it was a help to escape the hospital for a while and hold a little baby.

Days passed, all of this took about two weeks we all came together. I remember we were all in the room with him and he was awake. He couldn't talk because of the breathing tube, but he was very aware of who was there. He was touching each one of his fingers with his thumb on his right hand. I can still to this day see him doing it, I think all of us can. He would touch each finger with his thumb in order, index to pinky, like he was counting something. Although Dad never needed to count on his fingers, his brain was a computer, he used to do the times tables in his head just to entertain himself. At the time I am not sure any of us understood what he meant or why he was doing it but now we all know what he was trying to say, he was happy and excited that all four of his kids were there at his bed side, and by touching each of his fingers one at a time in order he was telling us that. I think Mom was the one who figured out what it meant a few years later. We still talk about him doing that, I know we all will never forget seeing him do that and love the meaning of it.

Over the next several day we continued waiting and watching and hoping things to get better. The doctors tried a few times to lower the settings on his breathing machine in hopes that he could do more breathing on his own. He could breath on his own, but he couldn't keep his $co2$ levels down, he couldn't exhale right, his muscular were too weak. They would turn the breathing machine down a level or two and his $co2$ level would rise and the Dad would drift back off into a coma and they would have to turn the machine back up. The doctor finally decided that he needed to talk to Mom and Dad about this. He told Dad and Mom in two separate conversations that he thought the Dad couldn't survive without the breathing machine and the only option he saw was to put a permanent one in his neck. But he said that he feel sure that Dad would be in such a weaken condition that he wouldn't be able to do anything but lie in bed, maybe not even keep his eyes open or talk. That is not a life for anyone, we knew that. So the next day we all came together around Dad's bed. The nurse had untied his right hand so he might be able to write his wishes down. He was tied down so he couldn't pull out any tubes. I don't remember if my grandmother was in the room with us then or not. She was at the hospital the whole time. I do remember her saying that she didn't want to see her son like that and that she would see him when he was all better. So we asked Dad what he wanted, he tried writing his feeling down with my younger brother help, but he couldn't see and his hand was shaking badly. Before long he started to get very upset and frustrated by the whole situation. The four of us left the room, Mom stayed a few extra minutes to calm him down as only she could do. The nurses knew this and never complained. The one thing that no one noticed was the nurse didn't tie his right hand back down. We all went back to the waiting room, confused and exhausted. It was decided that all of us except Mom and I would go home and run some errands and stuff. The two hours passed, everyone else was still gone, Mom and I started back to see Dad. As we walked back there, we could see nurses flying around and a ton of commotion going on around Dad's room. A nurse saw Mom and I and told us that he had pulled the breathing tube out. Mom stopped in the hall right outside his room, Dad was sitting up in his bed with his glasses on looking at us and an oxygen mask on his face. He was making this God awful coughing like noise, I can't begin to describe what it sounded like. One of my friends later called it the death rattle and I think he was right. Anyway, Mom stood there for a moment, I think she knew then she was losing him. She went to his side, she put one hand in his and the other around his head and she kissed him. I was standing at the foot of the bed and a nurse was standing on the other side. Mom said to Dad, "Dear darling, have you made a decision?" He shook his head yes and Mom said, "You realize this means you can't come home?" He shook his head yes again and then reached up and took the oxygen mask off his face and said in a very soft whisper to Mom, "I love you and no more, no more." Mom looked up at the nurse and said you understood that didn't you and she said yes through her tear. This was the most beautiful thing I have ever seen. The love between them filled the room. I will always feel honored that I got to witness that moment between them. Their last words of love to each other. It was the most beautiful thing I have or will ever see and and I will never forget that moment. I ran out of the room into the hall to the phone. I called the house and my younger brother answered the phone, I told him to get everybody back up to the hospital, that Dad had pulled the breathing tube out.

They all came back up there, I know that we were all with him one more time before he went into coma, but I don't remember again if my grandmother was there in the room or not. The hospital gave us our own private waiting room so we could talk about what we wanted to do now. We all agreed that Dad had made his decision and that we should stick to it. Up to this point I had been trying with everything I had to be strong, especially for Mom, but now I just couldn't do it anymore. I remember getting up and running out of the room. I don't remember where I went exactly. I was crying and very upset. I remember being in the hall somewhere in the hospital when this family who we had gotten to know a little in the waiting room over the last week or so came down the hall. They asked if I was okay and I told them that my father was dying. They tried to be as comforting as they could, bless their hearts. I wonder now whatever happened to them. I know that none of us remember their names or their story. It is strange how sometimes you meet people like that and they just disappear from your life. I went back to where Mom and all were. My sister said we were looking for you and wondering where you went. The doctor told us that he was having Dad moved from intensive care to a private room upstairs where we could be with him. The doctor knew that if he ordered Dad moved upstairs to a private room, the insurance would pay for it. After what seemed like forever, they got Dad upstairs in a private room, by this point he was in coma because of his co2 level was way too high. The room was very nice with a lazy boy like chair and a couch and a couple of other small chairs as well. I know there was a window as well, but I couldn't even begin to describe what was outside that window. We all collected together in the room with Dad. My grandmother in the lazy boy chair and the rest of us around the room. I sat in a chair next to Dad's bed for most of the night and held his hand. My younger brother sat on the other side of the bed and held the other hand. I can't tell you what we talked about that night. I remember going down to the chapel in the hospital a couple times and just sitting there by myself, thinking and crying. I asked the good Lord to be with Dad and take care of him. I remember feeling like my whole world was just going to end. That there was not going to be this huge hole that no one could ever fill. I remember thinking about all the things that I would never get to do with Dad. The biggest would be walking with him on my wedding day. I also thought about the stuff that I think everyone thinks about, you know, was I the person he wanted me to be, was he proud of me, that kind of stuff. My mother's mom went to her grave worried if she had lived up to her father. Mom and I joked about it not to long ago. Mom said that the only person I had to live up to was me. We sat there with Dad all night. They came in a couple times and checked on how things were, but they mostly just left us alone. We sat together all night. Early the next morning, everyone left the room for whatever reason. I ended up in the room alone with Dad. I walked up beside his bed and touched his hand. I told him not to hold to this for us, we would be okay. I told him that we would take care of Mom and I promised him that I would take care of my older brother and my grandmother. I leaned down and kissed his forehead and told him to go haunt Jerry Jones. He is the owner of the Dallas Cowboys and my Dad didn't like him at all. I also told Dad to go watch the Texas Rangers play ball and have the best seat in the house. Finally I said, "Goodbye Daddy I will always love you." After that everyone came back into the room. That morning was October 4th, my 33rd birthday. The doctor had told us the day before that he thought the Dad would survive the night but probably not the next day. That morning the two nurses who had helped care for him and had become very close to Mom and Dad, they came in and sat with us and we talked and laughed a little. I remember one of the was talking about the time when she had been taking care of him and he was in a kind of a cranky mood. I was home visiting on vacation at the time. When this nurse was finished and getting ready to leave. She and my Mom were standing, they were about to walk to the front door. Dad was complaining about everything that day, let's just say he was not in a good mood. I think before she knew what was coming out of her mouth, the nurse said out loud, "You cranky old fart!" She quickly covered her mouth and had this very shocked look on her face. We all laughed and laughed. Dad thought it was funny and it improved his mood for the rest of the day too. She could say something like that to him because he and Mom cared so much for those nurses. Those two women became very important members of our family. The very sad thing is none of us have any contact with them now. Even people who become so important to you can drift out of your life. We sat with Dad and remembered funny stories. I think I dozed a little in the chair I was sitting in, after all we were up all night. I really don't know exactly what time it was, but one of the nurses woke me up and said "Carol, he is gone." There was tears and hugs. I told one of the nurses that it was my birthday. We stood around his bed and said our goodbyes.

We left the hospital and went home. I remember going upstairs to my room and just laying on my bed and crying. I remember wishing that this was all a real bad dream and that I was going to wake up and none of it would be true. Mom came upstairs a few minutes later to see if I was okay. A week or so before the Dad got so sick and ended up in the hospital. He wanted to ordered a bunch of balloons and have them delivered to me for my birthday. I have always loved balloons. Mom told me about this and asked me if I still wanted the balloons. I said no because it just wouldn't be the same as it would be if Dad had done it. She understood. My best friend came into town and she was staying her aunt's house down the street. She and I have been friends for almost longer then I can remember. She asked me if I wanted to stay with her at her aunt's house that night. I remember asking Mom if she cared, she said she wanted me to do whatever I felt like doing and what made me happy. I stayed with her that night, I honestly don't remember anything we did or talked about that night. I do know that it was comforting and it helped me a lot to be with her. I don't think I have ever told her how much that night with her, just hanging out, being friends helped me. I hope when she reads this books she will finally know and how I will never forget. Our relationship is so special because we can always make each other smile and feel better no matter what the situation.

The next couple of days were spent calling old friends and making plans. I remember my sister and younger brother got the job of calling all of Dad's old oil field buddies. They would take turns and when one finish a call. He or she would say, "oh my gosh, that was tough, your turn." We would all laugh and remember Dad. My Dad passed away on my 33rd birthday. It took me several months before I could say that without falling apart. I have had people ask me how that makes me feel, if I was mad. No, I have ever been mad at Dad or at the good Lord, he didn't plan it that way, after all dying wasn't really what he wanted to do anyway. I must admit it has changed the way I feel about my birthday. Its hard for me, even to this day nearly eighteen years later, not to feel a little sad. I look at my birthday as a marker, it marks a passage of time. The funeral was great as funeral goes. Mom did her best to plan it so that it was a celebration of his life. The minister told two funny stories about the Dad. He came to see us so he could learn about the Dad and what we wanted him to say. One of the stories he told was one I told him about the time the Dad and I were driving my little Ford Escort home from my grandmother's house in a snow storm. This was a pretty nasty storm, wind blowing hard and the snow flakes were huge and heavy. Anyway the Dad and I got off I-40, which runs through the middle of Amarillo, and were almost home when the car got a flat tire. I was driving, we pulled into a parking lot of a bank and stopped. The Dad looked at me and said, "Well, Carol A., I think we have two choices, we can either leave the car and walk home or we can fix the flat tire?" We didn't know then what was wrong with Dad and as I look back on this event, I am very glad I said lets fix the flat, because I don't think he would have been able to make it home. Well we were at moment about ten blocks from the house and it was freezing cold and snowing like crazy. Like I have said before, this long before the average person had a cell phone and because of the storm everything was closed. I told Dad that I wanted to fix the flat. He agreed and we got out of the car and found the jack and the spare and all. When we were trying to set the jack up, it kept slipping on the ice. We couldn't get it to stay put and my Dad was slowly losing his religion as my mother says. I suddenly had this idea, I took my hat that I wore for work at the pizza place and put it under the jack. It worked, the jack stayed put and we changed the tire and went home. I remember the Dad saying when I stuck the hat under the jack, "Way to go, Carol A!" He called me Carol A a lot, my middle name is Ann. I can still hear him saying it. The other story the minister told that day was one my sister told him about when the Dad was teaching her how to drive and they ran out of gas. No one tells this story better then my sister, it is so funny. Needless to say they were able to find a phone and called Mom.

After the funeral, the church gave us a wonderful lunch with everyone who attended the services. It was great to see all the people who loved the Dad and all of us. The next couple of days after the funeral were spent just being together, supporting and loving each other. When things were settled I had to return to work. Leaving that day was one of the hardest things I had to do. I can't remember ever being as sad as I was that day. All I wanted to do was stay with Mom and my grandmother, but I knew I couldn't, I had return and do my job.

CHAPTER NINE

LEAVING THE PERFECT FAMILY

When I returned I started working on pulling things together for my resume. I had told the parents in May of 96 that I would be leaving in May of 97, I gave them a years notice. Why you ask, because they deserved it and it gave all of us time to get ready. The holidays came before I was even near ready for them. My Mom decided that she wasn't able to have Thanksgiving at home in Amarillo. So we all decided to meet at my sister's in Florida. I usually don't travel home for Thanksgiving because there is really not enough time, but this time I was pretty much required to be there. I have pictures of all of us together there at my sister's. We all look like we have just lost our best friend or something, they are really sad pictures. Christmas was home at Mom's in Amarillo. I just remember how strange it was to be in the house and not have the Dad there, sitting in his chair with his glasses on his head reading a book. Christmas that year was hard to say the least, but one funny thing was Mom made pumpkin pies like she does every year. Anyway, she wasn't herself and forgot to put sugar in when she made the pies. I remember tasting them, all of us wondering why they tasted so horrible. Mom finally realized what she forgot to add. We discovered that if you put enough cool-whip on it, it was okay. We all laughed about it now. Early that spring I contracted nanny agencies about getting another job.

One of the agencies I contacted presented me with a job that she said no one else wanted at all. It was with a family expecting triplets, yes triplets! I don't think I have to tell you what I did. I said, "Cool, how fast can you send them my information." I told her that I looked at this job with triplets as a wonderful challenge. She laughed at me and said okay I will let her know about you right away. I went home and told the parents about this new family expecting triplets and how much I really wanted that job. They too thought I was nuts and couldn't imagine caring for three babies all at the same time. I did have other families that I interviewed with, but all I could think about was the triplets. Finally I got a call from the mother who was still expecting the babies and was home on bed rest. We arranged an interview and that was that, I got the job. I began to tell the boys what I was about to do. I told them that they were big school boys now and these new babies needed me more then they did now. I told them that I wasn't moving far away and I would see them on weekends and such and that I would forever love them, both of those boys have now graduated from college. May came and they got a new nanny, I showed her the ropes, the boys did well with her, so I moved out. I said goodbye to the perfect family and wondered if I was making a mistake. The future is about change, I knew I had to move forward with the future. Would I ever find another family like them, was there another perfect family? I didn't know but I knew I was very excited about the triplets and the challenges they would bring. As I left the house that had been my home for three years. The house where the perfect family lived, I left like I was leaving my home again for the first time. I was happy and excited and scared and sad all at the same time.

CHAPTER TEN

TRIPLETS, THE BEGINNING

I moved into the triplets home just before the triplets were born. The father who is amazing had finished the attic so that I would have a room and a bathroom to myself. I call the father amazing because he is a paraplegic and in a wheelchair. I quickly learned that there was nothing that he couldn't do and he wasn't handicapped. The triplets were born on the 19th of June by c-section. Two boys and a girl, the girl was born first. She weight in at five pounds, three ounces, the middle boy was the smallest of the three. He weight in at three pounds, eight ounces and the other boy was the biggest, he weight in at five pounds, ten ounces. The grandparents took me with them up to the hospital the next day to see the babies. The little girl and the big boy were in the room with mother. The little boy was in NICU. I held the little girl, you could tell she was a girl just by looking at her pretty little face. The big boy is a copy of his father. I remember he had a dirty diaper, I was only one in the room who had the foggiest idea what to do about it. The father then took me down stairs to see the little guy. He was lying in a bassinet and was wide awake and wiggling like crazy. I noticed right away how alert and aware he was of the world around him. He had wiggled so much that one of his tiny arms came out of the sleeve of his shirt. You know one of those tiny little undershirts that hospitals put on babies. He was so little that that little shirt swallowed him. I carefully put his little arm back in his shirt and I talked to him a little. Then I took a picture of him with my polaroid camera so the mother could have a picture of him to hold. What amazing little guy, I was in love with all of them instantly, but you knew that already, right? The parents and I had worked out before the babies were born that they really didn't need me until August because of all the family that was there.

So I went home to Amarillo again to see Mom and my grandmother and all. Of course all I did was so off the pictures I had of the triplets and brag about them. I remember several of my mother's friends at church asking me if I really understood what I was getting myself into. I just laughed at them and told them that I was excited and couldn't wait to get started taking care of them. The month went by pretty quickly and I returned to the babies. For the first two weeks or so, the mother and I did it together, then she had to return to work and I was on my own. I remember that first day like it was yesterday. I was nervous and excited and there were these butterflies in my stomach the size of bats, but I knew that I could handle anything. both the mother and the father made sure I had everything I needed and know all of the phone numbers if needed. Finally they went out the door and me and the trio started our adventure together. The first few days were spent getting the babies on some sort of schedule. I had to work out how to fee three babies all at the same time. Two of which had issues with feeding. The baby girl had reflux and would throw up an entire bottle if you weren't careful. And the little baby boy had acid reflux and you had to feed him while holding him sitting upright so he could eat without pain. The doctor put these two on medicines to control the reflux and things did get somewhat better. The baby girl was still having major issues with reflux though. One day while I was watching them, she was sitting in her bouncy seat sleeping. She all of a sudden she tensed up, her body got tight, her little fist went up by her head and her knees were pulled up. I said whats going on? And I quickly picked her up. She coughed and choked a little and threw up all over. It was after that the doctors put her on a apnea monitor and she would sleep at night in her bouncy seat in their bedroom. It's hard to remember in what events happened, because around the same time when the babies were about four months old. One of the boys got very sick with whooping cough. He ended up in the hospital with iv's in both hands and on oxygen. He was in there for three or four days. All three babies had health issues at one time or another. But most of our days in the early days were spent having bottles, changing diapers and naps. One of my favorite thing to do was to lay out a big blanket on the floor. Then I would spread out the toys and have everything necessary to change a diaper if needed. Then I would get the cd player and lay the babies side by side on the blanket in front of me. I would turn on some kids tunes and sing along to the babies, usually making some stuff animal dance and sing in the air above them at the same time. This activity would usually produce kicks and wiggles and smiles. We would have more fun doing this most of the early morning. I surprised myself because I was able to get all three of them on the same schedule. Morning nap was at about ten if I remember right and it was only an hour or so. Then we were up, diaper changes of course and a bottle. If the weather was nice, I would load them up in the huge stroller and go for a walk. There was a large retirement and nursing home place down the street from the house. I remember walking down there and walking in front of the full care nursing home building. There was always some old folks sitting outside in wheelchairs. They especially the old ladies would go nuts over the babies. Oh I can't leave out a very special person from this story. The father had gotten to know this lady who lived across the backyard. She was a grandmother and was so excited about the babies. She quickly became one of my best friends. She would appear at the back door almost everyday and she would come in and see the babies and sit and hold and rock one of them. One of the boys and her soon became very close snuggle buddies. I loved it when she would appear because she gave me a chance to have an adult conversation during the long day plus that she was a lot of help too.

Time seem to fly by and before long they were sitting up and rolling around. One of my favorite memories, the mother got them what I called jolly jumpers. You know what I am talking about those things that hang in a door way and the baby sits in it and can jump and bounce. Anyway she got two of them and one day we had both of the boys in them. One of the boys really loved it from the word go and would bounce and swing like crazy and he had this yell he would do. It was he is happy yell, but it sounded painful and it was painful to everyone else ears for sure. The mother called it his terradactal yell, that always used to make me laugh. Anyway on this particular day, the boys were bouncing together and laughing at each other. The loud one was bouncing at his brother like a little bull frog and they were both giggling and having so much fun. The mother and I laughed and I think we got tears in our eyes because it was one of those moments. You know the ones that only happen once and if you are not careful you can miss them. The little girl never really enjoyed the jolly jumpers because of her tummy. She could sit and play, she loved balls. Which is pretty funny now, because now at nearly seventeen, she is awesome soccer and basketball player. She loved it if you would roll the ball to her and she could roll it back to you. She would get so excited, her little hands and feet going ninety miles at minute. She would cry if it rolled away and she couldn't get it.

The middle boy who was the smallest of the three would commando crawl everywhere. It always amazed me how fast he could go when he wanted to. The other boy could crawl on his hands and knees and he learned the fine art of getting into things first and soon taught this skill to his brother. I was forever pulling the two of them out from under the table or out of a kitchen cabinet or something. The little girl was so funny, she would get upset if one of the her brothers crawled out of her sight, even if it was only behind the couch. By the time they were ten months old she had figured out how this crawling thing worked and she was off after her brothers and that beloved ball. In the afternoon I would usually have walker time, yes I said walker time. This is before everyone discovered how dangerous they were. But we had three of them, the little girl hardly ever moved from the spot where I put her. The boys were a completely different story. The smaller boy learned how to cruise around in his walker real fast. The bigger boy had to work to keep up and would often get mad because he couldn't. I didn't enjoy walker time at all. I was constantly bending down to pick up toys they had thrown off their trays or something. It usually some sort of controlled chaos. I guess that was the way most things were when you are taking care of triplets.

CHAPTER ELEVEN

1ST YEAR

The first year flew by and before I knew it we were planning their first birthday party. The trios birthday is in June so we could count on good weather. The party was planned for the Saturday after their birthday. There was a cupcake for each baby and cake for everyone else. We had wading pools and games and art projects for the older kids. I don't remember all the kids that came or how many people were there, but I do remember the backyard being full of adults and kids running around. Anyway, a couple of days before the party on the trio's actual birthday, we had a little party with just family and close friends. The mother had a cupcake for each of the kids. I think it was me who suggested that we take all of the babies clothes off except for the diaper when they had their cupcake. We also had planned to give each one of them a bath afterwards as well. So we sat them in their highchairs side by side, the little girl in the middle. We all sang happy birthday to them and I remember all of us laughing when we were singing happy birthday to the trio because everyone sang their names in a different order. Then we blew out the candle on each cupcake and let them have it. The boys wasted no time and instantly picked up the cupcakes and started eating and making a big mess. The little girl just sat there and watched her brothers inhale their cupcakes. They were quickly becoming extremely messy too. Everyone tried to encourage the little girl to pick up her cupcake and take a bite but she continued just to sit there and watch. Then suddenly she just lean down and without touching the cupcake with her hands, she took a big bite out of the top of the cupcake. We all roared with laughter and I know somewhere I have it on video. I know what you are thinking, Americas

Funniest Home Videos, right? I know we probably could have won a ton of money, babies always win. I think she did it at least one more time before she finally started usually her hands.

The Saturday after their birthday we had the big party for them. We set up wading pools and games and tables and such in the backyard. There was tons of food and oodles of presents for the trio. The party was fun but somewhat exhausting. After their birthday the rest of the summer was spent playing in the wading pool out on the deck. Which meant skinny dipping for the trio, they didn't skinny dip at their birthday party. We usually didn't mess with swimsuits and diapers would just fill up with water and fall apart. I don't think they had those swim diapers back then. The trio would go skinny dipping in the backyard wading pool every summer until they were at least 3 years old. I know that when they read this they will be mad at me for telling you that, oh well, they will get over it. Its not like I included pictures. They never seemed to care so I didn't either. By the end of that summer they were really working on walking and pulling up on everything that would stand still long enough. I was hoping that they would all be walking well enough to go trick or treating that Halloween. With most their milestones, they would do them in birth order, except for the gross motor ones. In that area, the little girl was always last to do it, be it rolling over, sitting alone or crawling and walking. That is until she discovered soccer when they were five and then she was the best. I think in early October they were all walking successfully. Their mom ordered costumes for them. One of the boys was Tigger and one was Barney and the little girl was Marie the cat from a Disney movie. I remember the day we got the costumes in the mail. The mom and I dressed them up in them to see how they fit. When we got Tigger all dressed up his brother was laughing at him so hard there was almost tears rolling down his cheeks. We put crinkled up newspaper in the tail of Barney so it would stick out right. Watching him walking away from you was so freaking funny, watching that tail sway back and forth as he walked like all toddlers do. Oh my gosh it still makes me laugh real hard when I think about it. We tried to teach them to say trick or treat, but that was asking a lot. I often wonder what little kids think about Halloween. Their parents dress them up in strange outfits and take them out in the dark to ring doorbells and get food. I know they have to think that all the adults around them have gone mad. Anyway Tigger quickly discovered that there was food in his little bucket so he began digging into a package of cheese crackers he got as we walked along. The trio discovered chocolate and all kinds of candy on that first Halloween. It was great and so much fun, I think it took us nearly a half hour just to do our little block. I don't know if they ever had those costumes on again after that. I have never asked the mom if she saved them. Soon of course came Christmas and the holidays. Everyone knows that little children make Christmas extra special. We took them to see Santa. The little girl screamed like crazy, but the boys didn't seem to mind too much. The triplets made a killing so to speak that year with all the stuff they got. I must admit I spoil them rotten myself. I remember their mother wanted them to learn the true meaning of Christmas. She wanted them each to get three presents like Jesus got from the three wiremen, but with the grandparents and all buying them everything under the sun, that was hard, almost impossible. The father liked the idea but he couldn't stick to it either. It was great seeing Christmas through the trio's eyes. I also remember the Christmas tree falling down at lest once that year. After the holidays, I began looking for some kind of play group for them. They needed to have friends and be social. I called this one mother's group and was quickly rejected, kind of rudely I might add when they discovered I was just a nanny. I tried another group, mothers of twins and triplets, they too turned me away for just being the nanny. I must tell you that I was very angered by them refusing to allow the trio to join in on their fun. I didn't think about the fact that they were refusing me as well, it just about the triplets and that they were refusing them. Finally I found this deal called the Parents Resource Center. I called them, I was prepared to be turned away again but to my amazement I wasn't. There were three centers close to us and we could go to any of them. There was a small yearly fee per family. They told me that we could go and meet the teacher and see what I thought. So I told the mother about what I had found and I told her how important it was for the trio to make and have friends. She agreed and said we should go and see what it was all about. The next day I packed the trio in the van and we went to this elementary school. I remember taking the trio out of the van and standing them one at a time on the sidewalk and telling them, "wait right there and wait for Carol." After I got them out and got the diaper bag, I said "okay come on follow me babies, let's go this way." The trio followed me, they were so very cute, I can't even begin to tell you. We walked in and down this long hall, the whole time I was telling the trio to come on and that this was going to be so much fun. Finally we arrived at a door to a class at the end of the hall. I opened the door and was greeted by this wonderful woman and a bright classroom filled with toys and things to do and little friends to play with. I told her about myself and the triplets, she was amazed. I didn't know then just how special that place was going to be to me and the trio. I learned that day that it was open every week day, each day at certain times. Each day there was free play, the parents were responsible for their children and were encouraged to take part and play with their kids. At eleven or so every morning, the teacher would say it was clean up time. We would all help the kids put the toys away and then we would sit in a circle on a rug. The teacher would get out her guitar and we would have circle time, singing songs and reading stories. The trio and I made so many friends at that place. I often think about families we met and became so close too. I wonder how those kids have turned out and what they are like, if they are as tall as the trio, who are taller than me now. Like I have said before but it is worth repeating now it is strange how people come in your life and stay a short time and then just drift away. I am sad to tell you that none of us have contact with any of those families today, but back then they were very important and were some of my best friends. The parent resource center not gave the trio their first school like experience, it gave them tons of love and friendship. It did the something for me and then some. The friends we made there soon became daily visitors at our house. On days when the weather was nice, the backyard was full of kids laughing, running and playing and cold rainy days the basement was filled with laughing and playing. I will never forget the laughs we had, one summer day we had made a water slide down the slide of the swing set in our backyard. The kids were sliding down and landing on this old mat we had. Anyway, one of our little friends went down the slide and bounced about three times on his little butt across that old mat. Like a stone skipping across a pond, it didn't hurt him and he thought it was as funny as his mother and I did, oh my gosh we laughed so hard. we celebrated birthdays and milestones together, we were there for each other in good times and bed. In fact on September 11th, I had friends come over to play so it was like a normal day. They were way to young to understand what was happening and why. We worked hard to shelter them from all the news about 9/11. The mother of their little friends felt the same way.

CHAPTER TWELVE

TERRIBLE TWOS TIMES 3

When the trio was about 18 months old I started home schooling them. I found this preschool home school online. It was great, they sent all kinds of things to work with kids. One of the trio's favorite things was an alphabet train to go on the wall. Everyday we would add a new train car with a new letter. They loved to sing the alphabet song and point to each letter as they sang, not always pointing to the right letter, but they got a A for effort. They learned the song and they learned what each letter looked like.

Oh one important fact, I am leaving out, around the trio's first birthday the father started working on finishing the basement. He started making a new big kitchen and family room and a full bathroom. He did as much of the work as he could do on his own, but he had some help from friends. I just remember the noise being almost impossible to tolerate. It seemed like it lasted forever but in August after the trio's second birthday, it was finished. The money and the time and all put some stress on the parents. That is when I noticed the tension in the house being thicker than normal. The kids second birthday party was much like the first. Wading pools, arts & crafts stuff and tons of kids. The morning of the kids second birthday, the tension between the parents all came to a head. They had a big fight, I am not sure what it was about or what started it but it was bad. I remember thinking to myself that if they ruin today, I would kill them myself. The parents settled their issues at least for the day and by the time the party started no one knew anything ever happened between them.

The trio and I continued going to the parent resource center and on adventures with our friends. One of their favorite places to go was Pets mart to see the fish and other animals. Going there was kind of like our little science class. We would talk about the fish, hamsters and birds and sometimes the lizards and snakes as well. The little girl had this unexplained fear of animals, especially dogs and cats. We couldn't figure why this fear developed, she was never bitten or anything, but she was very afraid of them. The mother had, at that time an old cat named Dagmar, who was old and kind of cranky, but wouldn't really hurt anyone. The little girl would scream and cry with fear any time that cat came anywhere near her. Anyway on this particular adventure, we were in the pet store walking around looking at different stuff. When all of a sudden we walked around this corner and the little girl came face to face with a great dane. She screamed loud enough to break your ear drums I swear. If you have ever met a great dane dog, you know how sweet natured they are. The little girl's screams and cries scared this poor dog to death, he couldn't for the life of him figure out what he had done to make this child scream at him so. The look on the dog's face and his master's face was priceless. The little girl turned and began to scale up me like I was a tree, screaming and crying all the way. What was extremely funny was both of the little boys were not the least bit afraid of this giant dog. The middle boys was standing beside the dog patting him and saying, "big doggy, big doggy!" I explained the situation to the dog's owner, who was at this point getting a real good laugh out of the entire deal. The man took the giant dog away, everyone stopped staring at us. I calmed the little girl down and convinced her that the world wasn't coming to an end. It was for me one of what some people call life's most embarrassing moments for sure. Kids are really good at those kind of things, getting everyone in a store to stare at you. I put her down and we continued where we left off. Yes, believe it or not I didn't leave the store. That is the difference between parents and nannies. Parents are more likely to leave after a situation like that, most parents anyway. There are exceptions to the rule of course. Nannies are usually better at resolving situations like that and moving on and not let it ruin everything. I guess nannies are better at distraction. After all that is what we get paid to do, right?

Our life in those days were made up field trips to places like the pet store and play dates with friends and school work at home and the parent resource center. As with most two year olds, our life also had the occasional melt down from at least one of the trio. Let me tell you, it takes a ton of patience and love to deal with three two years old having a melt down. I tried very hard to avoid that situation at all costs. When I tell people about the trio, I always tell them that I would love to turn back the clock and do it all over again. That is true, but there are certain parts that I might be willing to leave out. The melt downs are without a doubt something I would leave out. The little girl was already a clothes horse, she was by no means a girly girl, but she liked her clothes for sure. She would get crazy sometimes, if a little water got on her shirt. She would have a huge melt down when I wouldn't allow her to change clothes. You are thinking, it wouldn't be easier just to let her change clothes and avoid the melt down. Yes it would but think about the laundry that begins to build when she changes clothes three or four times a day. She and I eventually worked out a deal, I would put her shirt or whatever in the dryer for a few seconds and all her problems would be gone. The best day was when she got over this phase completely and small wet spots on her clothes didn't bother her at all anymore. The middle boy had his little people and action figures that he just had to take with him everywhere he went. This was always interesting, he always wanted to bring more of them with him than he could carry by himself. This would cause both of us problems, until one day I found this mini back pack that was perfect for carrying all of his little people in. I will never forget his face when I showed him how all of his favorite little people and action figures fit in it. He was so happy and so was I, one less thing to cause me stress. The other boy really didn't have many melt downs, he was the trouble maker of the three. Even at two, his favorite thing was to see how pissed off he could make his brother especially. My biggest problem with him was his very contagious belly laugh. If he was doing something like annoying his brother laughing all the way. It was very hard to maintain a straight face and not laugh right along with him. This chapter could go on forever, the stories are endless and I don't want to play favorites. The triplet section of the book can't be a lot longer than the other kids, thats not fair.

CHAPTER THIRTEEN

THE TRIPLETS, THEN AND NOW

When I started writing this book, I knew what stories to tell about all the other families I have care for, but when it comes to my trio, it is very hard. I mean I could write so many stories about the triplets that this book would never end. As I said before in this book, the marriage was falling apart. At this point I am walking on thin ice if you understand what I mean. I don't want to hurt anyone, they have all come full circle. So out of love for that wonderful family, I am going to leave out of this all the bad time. I left the trio in the spring of 02. I was gone for about a year, during that time I worked for two families. One family was a single mother with an adopted Russian little girl. My job mainly was to teach her english, which was easy, little kids pick up that stuff real fast. I am not sure if I remember exactly why the job didn't last, something to do with the single mother's family I think. The other nanny job I had was with a family with one little boy and expecting another baby. That job was my first real live out nanny job. It was great, I had my own apartment for a while. In the summer of 03 I got sick and ended up having to have surgery and the job ended. I have three families that I am no longer in touch with and those are two of them. After my surgery in the fall I went back to the trio who were now starting first grade. I was there for five more years. There were still some hard times, but for the most part things were good. Just being back with my trio again made everything better for me. The entire year I was away from them, all I could think about every day was the trio and what they were doing and what was happening with them. I have always been somewhat protective of my kids, but especially the trio.

Those five years were full of homework, soccer games, video games, birthday parties and friends. The trio and I helped each other through good time and bad. Playground battles, grades, music lessons and soccer practices and games, this what my life was filled with. When I came in late 2003, the triplets were in the first grade, with every school year came issues. In first grade the middle boy had issues with behavior, not bad just minor behavior issues. The school had this color code system, green meant good, yellow meant your behavior could be better and red meant bad and you were in trouble. The middle boy had trouble staying on green all day. The other two kids hardly ever did have this problem. Second grade was better, the boys were in the same class. The middle boy improved his act and learned how to stay on green. I think having his brother in the same class with him helped some, because he knew his brother would have no problem telling on him.

Oh my gosh I am leaving an important character out of this story. She entered our lives when the trio were about three years old. She was a beagle puppy named Lucy. Lucy was then and is today a very loud character. Barking is her favorite thing to do. She was then and still is crazy to some extent but she makes up for it all with a constant, unconditional supply of love. She is the sweetest dog, there is not a mean bone in her body. The little girl used to love to dress Lucy up in her doll clothes. Lucy would just fall over and refuse to move and the worst she would do to the little girl is lick her on the face and make her giggle. Growling and snapping at her was never an option for Lucy. She just loved the kids no matter what they did to her. The trio and I soon discovered Lucy's true love, balloons. You could blow up a balloon and tie a string on it and give it to Lucy. She would take the string in her mouth and run around and the best time playing with her balloon. If the kids had balloons, I had to make sure to give Lucy one as well or there would be tears from at least one of the kids, when Lucy stole their balloon. Lucy was also an explorer, if given the chance she loves to run off, nose to the ground and howling all the way. I remember many chases, I guess the best thing was that constant howling, if she was out of your sight, you always knew about where she was or in what direction she was headed in. Lucy is getting up there in age now and doesn't have the energy she used to. She still has a heart full of love. Lucy lives with the trio's mother. When the trio were about ten I think, a new member of the family was added. A dachshund puppy the kids named Daisy.

The trio's Dad grew up with dachshunds and loves them. Daisy is a little sort of fat fire ball. Daisy is a long haired with black and brown. She and Lucy get along well, but I think Daisy picks on Lucy some. I know Lucy is glad that they don't live together all the time. Daisy took to me quickly and became my little black shadow. She was always ready to go when I was taking the kids to school or going over to their mother's to help her. Riding on my lap with her front feet up on the steering wheel like she was doing the driving. I remember the father in the bathroom getting ready to go to work and the kids over at their mom's. I would come downstairs to go out the front door, Daisy would be right there by the door waiting to go. The father and I would talk about things through the door of the bathroom door, the days events usually and then with Daisy I would go over to the mother's. When we would get there, there was always several minutes of barking from both dogs. I guess they were talking, saying good morning and such. Then the kids and I would laugh when they would begin to play and chase each other around up and down the stairs and banking the couch. Crazy and loud but always good for a great laugh. For me what was even better was the giggles and smiles coming from the kids. One of the boys had the best belly laugh, he still does today, it is contagious. There is no way you can hear this laugh and not start laughing yourself. I could go on forever about the dogs and the giggles and everything.

One of the boys loved reptiles and wanted a snake. The father ordered this snake from somewhere and it came federal express. It was a little corn snake. I like snakes and was happy to help and teach the kids how to take care of him. The snake arrived while the kids were in school one day and the father put him in the aquarium we had set up. None of us knew that this little snake could get out but he did. The sad thing is this all happened while the kids were still in school, so the kids didn't even get to see it before it got away, they were very sad. We spent the next week or so looking for this little snake. All of us thinking he was under the refrigerator or the oven. Then one night before bedtime, I was helping the little girl look for something she had missed placed. I moved some pillows on the couch looking for this thing she wanted and there was the snake. I screamed, "I found the snake, I found the snake!" The boys and their father had gone upstairs, I picked up the snake. The father was upstairs, telling the boys to go downstairs and find out why in the world I was yelling. I took the snail upstairs and happiness began.

We had the snake for about a couple of months or so. I got a better tank top to prevent future escape and all as well. Then one day, I am not sure what happened or how, but the top wasn't on right and the snake escaped again, never to be seen again. After the snake came frogs, which they raised from tadpoles and the last of which died not that long ago.

Those years with the triplets were filled with so many happy and sad and somewhat crazy moments. Its hard for me to know where to begin or what stories to tell. I did leave in the spring of 02. The parents were going through a divorce. I grew up in a house full of love all the time. Seriously my only wish is to have all of my kids come and stay with me and my family for a while and be wrapped in the love that is my family. I guess I am spoiled and I know what you are saying, oh come join the real world and man up, right? Well I have to tell you in this situation that is easier said then done. Looking back on it now, I am glad I did leave because I was able to maintain a relationship with both parents. If I would have stayed, I would have had to chose sides between the mother and the father. I really did want to stay because I wanted to protect and help the trio deal with the craziness that was happening in their world. I am not sure I could have taken either her side or his side. When I did return in the fall of 03, the mother was worried about what my real reasons were for returning. She told me later that she was worried I was only there to help the father take the triplets away from her. I told both parents more then once that I was on the kid's side and that the kids and my unending love for them was the only reason I returned.

In the earlier chapter I talked about the perfect family. They were in many ways, but it really isn't fair for me to call them the perfect family. All of the families I have taken care of are perfect in their own way. The triplets family was perfect for me because they taught me so much about love, trust, understanding and forgiveness. My nanny skills were tested to the max when I was presented with three little babies that I had to care for by myself. I learned so much about dealing with relationships and communication. The relationship I had with the father of the trio was one of friendship, it was based on honesty and trust and communication. He and I were always able to talk about what was going on. With the issues between the parents, I had to learn the best way to communicate with them individually. My relationship with mother was great in the early days, we were very close and could talk about anything, but when I returned she didn't trust me and our relationship suffered. I was walking on ice with her, I had to earn her trust again. She and I both worked on rebuilding our relationship slowly. It was rocky for a while and I have to admit that there were times when I just wanted to pack it in and quit. I would think to myself that I could easily get a new nanny position without all the issues and trouble and maybe even more money. Then I would pick up those kids from the bus stop or something and all of those thoughts would disappear. I knew that if I stayed strong that things would get better for everyone, especially for the kids. I was right with time things did get better. The mother and I gradually improved our relationship, I slowly earned her trust back, it slowly got back to what it was when we first met. I must tell you that there is not a soul on this earth that I am more proud of then the mother of the trio. She had issues both physically and emotionally. She worked hard and over time she conquered it all. She got her life back together and became the best possible mother she could be to those kids. She started a new life for her and the kids and her house is full of love, trust, understanding and fun. I don't think I have ever told her any of this, but someday I will. Maybe she will read this book and that is how I will tell her. By the time the trio was in the fifth grade, things couldn't be better. The parents had come full circle and their relationship had improved as well. They were able to communicate without issue most of the time and even do things together and do things with the kids as a family. During that year I decided that I could leave, that the triplets would be okay. My job here was done, I had done what I set out to do, to help the family and care for the kids. The title of this chapter is the triplets then and now. The chapters in this would never end if I told you everything that happened in those 11 years of life with the trio. Now they are almost 17 and in the fall will be seniors in high school. They are driving and beginning to make plans for college. The girl is still an amazing soccer and basketball player. The middle boy who was only 3 pounds at birth, is now the biggest I think, he is in a naval cadet program at school. I have high hopes that he will someday go to the naval academy in Annapolis. Then I would have a kid who graduated from West Point and a kid who graduates from Annapolis, that would be way cool, right? The youngest boy has a girlfriend and still has the best belly laugh ever. For Christmas their father sent me a picture of the kids. It is one of them standing together, all dressed up to go to a dance. I told him then that it was the best present and it still is.

CHAPTER FOURTEEN

LIFE CONTINUES....

After I left the triplets I headed north to the Boston area. Since moving up here in the summer of 2008 I have taken care of three families. The first was in a little old town north of Boston called Newburyport. Wonderful place, full of history and beautiful especially in the fall. The family had one little girl when I started and a second little girl before I left. The positions lasted about six months. Failure to communicate was the reason, there was very little if any communication between me and the mother. I can't really explain what happened or why. The mother and I just never really connected for reasons I don't know or understand. The job started in July and in mid November, the parents and I had a talk about the situation and we all agreed that the best thing to do was to part company before things got bad between us. I know it wasn't totally my fault, after all it takes two people for communication, but I blame myself, I look at it as my failure. Communication is the key to a great working relationship between the nanny and the parents. I left in the first part of December, I decided to head to Mom's in Florida for the holidays. I made the trip home, stopping off in Maryland to see the triplets of course. Just before Christmas I got a call from a nanny agency about a family in Boston area with twin baby boys. After Christmas I got a call from the mother, she seemed nice and I liked her from the beginning. She made arrangement for me to fly up there for the day and interview. When I got there to meet this family, I remember thinking that these kids will probably want for nothing, the house was huge. The family was sweet, the baby boys were adorable. The mother was my favorite from the start, the father seemed distracted, like he had better things to do. I did get the job and loaded up the car again and drove all the way back up there, it took me about three days to make the journey. They had a great place for the nanny on the third floor of their house. It was like an apartment, it was huge, it had a big screen television in the living room area and a little kitchen, it wasn't a complete kitchen, there wasn't a stove. There was a nice size bedroom with the biggest walk in closest I have ever seen and a bathroom. I was with this family for almost three years. It was great, the last year was rough and the reason I left. The mother got very ill and nearly died and the hours I was working got longer and longer. It is a long story and one that is still painful for me to tell. I haven't talked to or haven't seen this family since I left in early Sept 2011. For me leaving this family was more heartbreaking then leaving any other family, including the triplets. The mother's illness changed her and our relationship, we didn't get along and there was distance between us that wasn't there before. It isn't anyone's fault and I can't explain it to you. I didn't know how to fix it and that bothers me to this day. I not only lost the boys, I also lost a friend. So I left and stayed with friends for a while and I must be honest with you at this point. I wish with all that I have that I would have just packed up and left Boston and went back to DC or back to Mom's in Florida, but I didn't. A friend tells me about this couple she knows who are looking for a nanny, a live out nanny. They called me and I went to meet them and interview. Before I continue any farther, just let me say that these parents who were new parents and new to the world of nannies, had the very best communication skills ever. The three of us were always on the same page, if not we could easily get there. This position lasted two and a half years. They had twin girls who were 7 months when I started and nearly three years when I left. The girls were adorable and soon had the key to my heart. They both have amazing blue eyes, blue eyes that make you look twice at them. I struggled while I was working with this family mainly with keeping a roof over my head. The parents were wonderful to me, they did everything possible to help me including letting me stay with the grandmother down the street. I finally found a place, a little farther away from work then planned but it worked for a while. I was there for two and a half years and left when the girls were ready for school. The mother found a great preschool/daycare for them. I miss them very much but they are doing so well and are very happy and I talked to them often. You have to know that the reason I stayed through all of the struggles of finding a spot to live was the faces of those two little girls. They would greet me at the door every morning with a hi and a big smile and a hug and those amazing eyes.

FOR ALL OF MY
FAMILIES IN THIS BOOK

First of all, I want to say thank you to all of the parents for letting me be apart of your children's lives, to live in your homes, to be a part of your family life. I have a life time of memories that could fill ten books, all of which I cherish more then words can say. It was a privilege and an honor. I have always felt that I should have been paying you instead of you paying me, because I got to see and be apart of so much and was the recipient of so much unconditional love. I remember and cherish every smile, giggle, hug and kiss. I hope that when read this book you can see things from both sides and the importance of communication and understanding. I hope you can feel the love I had and still do have for your kids. When I say my kids, that is what I mean. All of my kids will forever hold a key to my heart, whether I have contact with them or not. When I started writing my adventures down it was for my own sake. In the beginning I never planned on sharing it with anyone. Time went by and adventures got added and it got better and I finally decided that it was time to make it a book. I found a publisher that wants to publish it. So here it is a book, a book about you and me and your kids and our lives together. I hope you remember all the stories I tell in the book. I hope you can love, laugh and cry as you read. I hope you will learn more about me that you didn't know before.

The biggest lesson I learned as a nanny was acceptance. Children accept you at face value, I wish adults could do that. That is what your kids did for me. I sure you have noticed that I didn't mention any names in the book. Two reasons, permission from you, that I didn't have and second privacy, your kid's privacy and yours. I think that I wouldn't have used names even if I had your permission, because the protector in me won't allow it. I have and always will protect my kids like a mother grizzly bear with a thorn in her paw. In the book I talk about how my father didn't like the people I worked for, because he believed that if you had a kid, you should take care of and raise the kid yourself, not hire some stranger to come in and do it for you. Please understand that he was a product of his time and place, like me he grew up in small town Texas, nannies are something that was new to me when I started and new to him. Only one family had the privilege to meet my Dad and for that I am sorry. I know for sure that he would have changed his attitude completely had he had the chance to meet you all. The Dad would have been amazed and very proud of all of my kids and the things they do and the amazing people they are becoming. My family is constantly asking me for pictures and stories about my kids. Just know that my family, especially my Mom loves your kids as much as I do. Grandchildren is something that she got cheated out on, she only got one, so she looks at all of my kids as step grandkids. She loves them, they all have a grandma that lives in Florida. Finally to all of my kids, most of you can now read this book yourself. I hope I didn't embarrass you to badly and I hope you remember all the laughter and the tears. I know that there are several stories that I didn't include, I did that for several reasons, the biggest one is I didn't want the book to be a thousand pages long and I have to save some material for a possible second book right? I want to thank you too for all of unconditional love, giggles, smiles, hugs, kisses and tears. I cherish every moment we spent together, good or bad. There is no one in the world who is more proud of you than me. I hope you have also learned something, like the importance of communication and understanding with parents, friends and an old nanny who loves you very much. I have a dream that someday I can have a reunion with all of my kids and their families. So that all of us together can share the stories and laugh. As you, my kids become adults and go out into the world, go after your dreams. Set your sights on what you want to do with your life and go get it. My hope is someday to be sitting in my rocking chair and see you on television or in the newspaper and say that's my kid! My heart truly belongs to all of you and it always will. Like I said once in this book, I wish I could turn the clock back and do it all again. The only thing I would change is for the time not to go by so fast. I wish I could go back and enjoy all of those special moments and take notice of the ones I missed the first time.

I love you all!!!